UNIVERSITY LIBRARY
UW-STEVENS POINT

35.00
70c

D1271081

UNIVERSITY LIBRARY
DUNDEE FIFE CONT

Saltmarsh Ecology

TERTIARY LEVEL BIOLOGY

A series covering selected areas of biology at advanced undergraduate level. While designed specifically for course options at this level within Universities and Polytechnics, the series will be of great value to specialists and research workers in other fields who require a knowledge of the essentials of a subject.

Saltmarsh Ecology

S. P. LONG, B.Sc., Ph.D.
C. F. MASON, B.Sc., D.Phil.

Lecturers in Biology in the
University of Essex

Blackie

Glasgow and London

Distributed in the USA by
Chapman and Hall
New York

Blackie & Son Limited
Bishopbriggs, Glasgow G64 2NZ

Furnival House, 14–18 High Holborn, London WC1V 6BX

Distributed in the USA by
Chapman and Hall
in association with Methuen, Inc.
733 Third Avenue, New York, N.Y. 10017

© 1983 Blackie & Son Ltd
First published 1983

All rights reserved.
No part of this publication may be reproduced,
stored in a retrieval system, or transmitted,
in any form or by any means,
electronic, mechanical, recording or otherwise,
without prior permission of the Publishers

British Library Cataloguing in Publication Data

Long, S. P.
　　Saltmarsh ecology — (Tertiary level biology)
　　1. Tidemarsh ecology
　　I. Title　　II. Mason, C. F.　　III. Series
　　574.5′2636　　　QH541.5.S24

　　ISBN 0-216-91439-6
　　ISBN 0-216-91438-8　Pbk

Library of Congress Cataloging in Publication Data

Long, S. P.
　　Saltmarsh ecology.

　　(Tertiary level biology)
　　Bibliography: p.
　　Includes index.
　　1. Tidemarsh ecology.　　I. Mason, C. F.
　　II. Title.　　III. Series.
　　QH541.5.S24L66　1983　　574.5′2636　　　82-17833
　　ISBN 0-412-00301-5 (Chapman & Hall)
　　ISBN 0-412-00311-2 (Chapman & Hall: pbk.)

Filmset by Advanced Filmsetters (Glasgow) Ltd.
Printed in Great Britain by Bell and Bain Ltd., Glasgow

QH
541.5
.S24
L66
1983

Preface

Coastal salt marshes form some of the largest tracts of semi-natural and unspoilt habitat in the developed countries of the west. Even in heavily industrialized estuaries, salt marshes often remain in a surprisingly natural state. They contain ecologically and physiologically interesting communities, where the distributions of marine and terrestrial organisms overlap. Colonizers from marine habitats are presented with severe problems caused by desiccation, while terrestrial organisms must adapt to periodic submergence. All organisms must adapt to the wide fluctuations in salinity on the salt marsh. A superficial glance at a salt marsh might suggest a rather uniform environment, inhabited by few species. Closer examination reveals a mosaic of distinct micro-habitats, with their own associations of highly adapted plants and animals.

The value of salt marshes extends beyond their boundaries. Much of the high yield of plant material may be washed by tides into coastal waters, fuelling marine food chains, including commercial fisheries. Salt marshes are also valuable in coastal defence, reducing the energy of waves by frictional drag, and protecting terrestrial resources from the ravages of the sea. At the same time, salt marshes are under increasing threat due to pollution and to reclamation for agriculture, industry and leisure.

Much early research on salt marshes concentrated on the zonation and succession of vegetation. The last two decades, however, have seen a rapid widening in our knowledge of the dynamics of processes in salt marshes. Most of the research has been done in North America and Western Europe. In the former, emphasis has been placed on ecosystem dynamics, while the latter has concentrated on species distribution. Both have been concerned with conservation. This text compares and integrates information on these two geographic zones.

The introductory chapter defines the salt marsh, examines the global distribution and describes the overriding influence of the tidal cycle. The following three chapters consider the physical habitats, their plants and

362227

animals. Teal's pioneering work on saltmarsh dynamics has stimulated a wealth of research on production, decomposition and nutrient cycling, which is considered in Chapters 5 and 6. The final chapter examines the threats to salt marshes, and their conservation.

We hope that this text may encourage readers to explore salt marshes for themselves. Salt marshes often represent the last real wilderness areas close to many of our large cities, but they will only be conserved if a wider audience is made aware of their value, their beauty and the many problems with which modern man besets them.

We would like to thank Ann Long and Sheila Macdonald for reading the manuscript and Vivien Amos and Kathleen Stock for typing it.

S.P.L.
C.F.M.

Contents

CHAPTER ONE

INTRODUCTION

1.1 Significance and definition

In some of the most populous and most heavily industrialized areas of the developed world, salt marshes are among the few remaining habitats that have not been markedly altered by man. Examples include the salt marsh of much of the New England coast, San Francisco Bay, the southern coast of the Netherlands and the Essex coast near to London. In his novel *The Snow Goose* (Michael Joseph, [1941] 1969) Paul Gallico describes the salt marshes close to London:

> one of the last wild places of England, a low, far-reaching expanse of grass and half-submerged meadowlands ending in the great saltings and mudflats near the rest-less sea... it is desolate, utterly lonely, and made lonelier by the calls and cries of the wild birds that make their homes on these marshes.

Anyone who has spent a few hours alone on a coastal salt marsh will know how perfectly these words capture the atmosphere of these places. Yet salt marshes, so often taken for granted, exist by a delicate balance of biological and physical factors not fully understood, but all too easily disturbed by man. The current understanding of these habitats forms the subject of this book.

The Oxford English Dictionary defines salt marsh as "marshland over-washed by the sea". A more complete definition reflecting the biological and physical attributes of salt marsh would be areas of alluvial or peat deposits, colonized by herbaceous and small shrubby terrestrial vascular plants, almost permanently wet and frequently inundated with saline waters.

This definition sets the limits on the subject of this book. It may well seem verbose for a description of a habitat known to many, yet it is necessary to clearly separate it from the many other habitats which share some of its features. Rocky shores are separated, their deposits being ancient or igneous. Mudflats, eelgrass (*Zostera* sp.) beds and mangroves differ in that their vegetation is respectively algae, aquatic flowering plants, and shrubs or trees. Salt deserts are separated since, although saline

1

Figure 1.1   An oblique aerial view of the 400 ha salt marsh of Colne Point, E. England. This is a lagoonal marsh which has formed landward of the protecting shingle ridge seen on the right of the picture. The major drainage channel, running through the centre of the marsh, serves numerous tributaries which branch to ramify throughout the marsh. Variations in shade over the marsh surface reflect zonation of the vegetation. (Photo: Aerial Photography Unit, Cambridge University; copyright reserved.)

habitats, they are not permanently wet and may endure frequent and long periods during which potential evapotranspiration exceeds water gain. The requirement in the definition of frequent inundation by saline waters suggests a coastal habitat, but it does not rule out inland salt marshes, such as areas adjacent to saline lakes of frequently fluctuating level and areas irrigated by saline springs. This text, however, is primarily concerned with coastal salt marsh. Where salt water is diluted by fresh water from the land, as in river estuaries, saltwater and freshwater marsh will intergrade. Since all natural waters must contain some salts, however little, the requirement that the inundating water should be saline may seem ambiguous. The difference between fresh water and salt water has therefore to be one of quantities of dissolved salts. A useful dividing line is an average salt concentration of $5\,\mathrm{g\,l^{-1}}$ in the inundating water, since below this concentration salt-tolerant plants (halophytes) are replaced by plants typical of non-saline soils (glycophytes) in temperate regions.

1.2 Tidal range

Anyone who has observed a steep rocky shore at low water will have noticed the distinct banding of lichens, algae and molluscs which correspond to different tide heights. Tide heights are similarly important to the ecology of saltmarsh organisms. A clear banding of flowering plant species may be found on some salt marshes, although this pattern is more often obscured by undulations in a gently sloping surface and by horizontal variation in soil characteristics. Typically, salt marshes will contain three zones of flowering plants and their associated communities. At the lowest levels a sparse growth of a few species forms the pioneer zone or low marsh. This intergrades at higher levels with the richer flora of the mature zone or middle marsh. Finally, the species of the mature zone are partially replaced at the highest level of the salt marsh or high marsh by species of non-saline habitats or facultative halophytes which can only withstand brief and infrequent submergence in sea water.

The use of relative tide height rather than actual altitude is generally more meaningful in the ecology of intertidal shores. The communities found around the high tide mark at different locations will show greater similarity than the communities found say at 1 m above mean sea level regardless of tidal range. This is because frequency and duration of submergence is a major influence on the composition of intertidal communities. For any given shore, positions with respect to tides may be defined by the heights of low and high tide as related to a reference point. In Britain this reference is mean sea level at Newlyn, Cornwall, i.e. the mean of high and low water recorded at Newlyn over several years (Dury, 1972). Its use in tide tables and records is denoted as Ordnance Datum (O.D.) Newlyn.

Superimposed on the familiar tidal cycle of *c*. 12.5 h frequency (Fig.

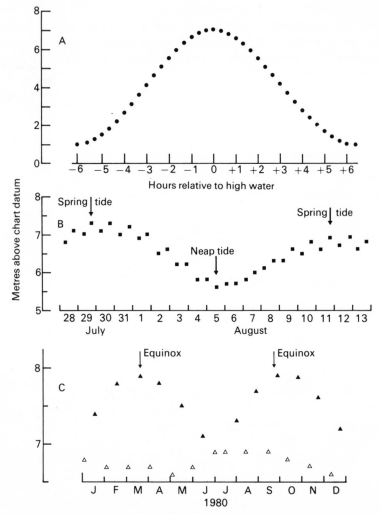

Figure 1.2 Predicted tide heights in Milford Haven, S.W. Wales. (A) One tidal cycle (1 Aug. 1980); (B) all high tides over 18 days (28 July–14 Aug. 1980); (C) all spring tides during 1980. Closed symbols denote the highest spring tide of each calendar month. Chart datum (LAT) in Milford Haven stands at 3.71 m below O.D. (Newlyn). Data from Admiralty (1980).

1.2*A*) are two-weekly and six-monthly cycles, besides longer cycles of several years. Once in every two weeks tidal amplitude, i.e. difference between low and high tides, will reach a maximum, known as spring tide. The amplitude of the tides following the spring tide will decrease over 7 days to a minimum known as the neap tide and will then increase again over the next 7 days back to another spring tide to complete the cycle (Fig. 1.2*B*). The amplitudes of the spring and neap tides are not constant throughout a year. At any given location the greatest amplitude occurs in the spring tide closest in time to the equinoxes, the smallest occurring at the solstices (Fig. 1.2*C*). The equinoctial spring tides vary slightly in amplitude from year to year in accordance with slight changes in the relative positions of the sun, moon and earth. The extreme tides that can be

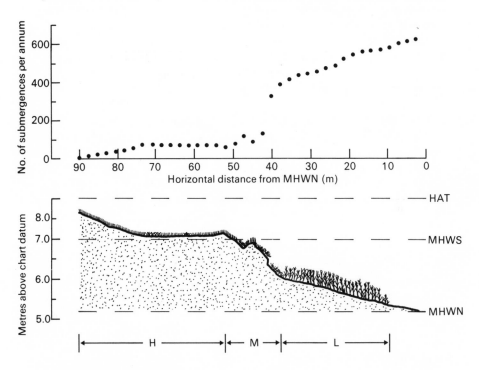

Figure 1.3 Profile of the salt marsh at Bentlass in Milford Haven, S.W. Wales. Low marsh (L) dominated by *Spartina anglica*, middle marsh dominated by *Puccinellia maritima* or mixed communities including *Armeria maritima* and *Plantago maritima*, and high marsh (H) dominated by *Festuca rubra* (after Dalby, 1970). The number of submergences per annum for points along the transect are indicated in the graph above the profile.

produced on any shore through astronomical events are known as the highest (HAT) and lowest (LAT) astronomical tides. These points, together with the mean levels of high water averaged over several years of tide height recording of all spring tides (MHWS), all tides (MHW) and all neap tides (MHWN), provide useful reference points when considering the distribution of saltmarsh communities. At Bentlass salt marsh in Milford Haven, S.W. Wales (Fig. 1.3), the low marsh begins just above MHWN, middle marsh at about MHW and high marsh at MHWS, each point being marked by a vegetational change. Comparison of these levels with tide heights in Milford Haven (Fig. 1.2) shows that whilst most of the 700 or so tides a year will reach the lowest part of the marsh, the highest levels at about 7.5 m above chart datum will only be reached by the equinoctial spring tides (Fig. 1.2C). Since tidal cycles are dependent on regular astronomical events they show consistency throughout the world. In contrast, tidal range in coastal waters varies greatly since local geographical variation can dampen or amplify the tidal range of the oceans. On a world scale, tidal range varies from c. 16 m in the Bay of Fundy, S.E. Canada, to 30 cm on the Baltic coast of Sweden (Ranwell, 1972). Even within Britain the difference between MHW and MLW ranges from 9.4 m at Avonmouth in the Bristol Channel to 1.2 m at Lerwick in Shetland (Admiralty, 1980).

The tide heights considered so far are those that could be expected by averaging past records, and reflect changes in the gravitational pulls of the sun and moon on the oceans. Unpredictable and extreme weather conditions such as storms, hurricanes, deep atmospheric depressions, long periods of continuous rain or a sudden thaw may considerably alter these predicted tide heights in coastal waters, particularly if the local geography serves to accentuate the weather effects. For example, in the North Sea, severe northerly storms funnel water southwards towards the narrow exit at the straits of Dover, causing water levels to rise in the southern North Sea, so that tide heights may be up to 2 m above those predicted from astronomical events. Occasionally, astronomical events and storms may combine to produce an exceptionally high tide, as in 1953 when the sea temporarily claimed back thousands of hectares of reclaimed tidal flat and salt marsh with much loss of life in both E. England and the Netherlands. It is during such storms that the major changes to coastal form may occur and their frequency and duration also have an important influence on the distribution of salt marsh.

By definition salt marshes must bear higher terrestrial plants and these can only colonize shores which are sheltered from the full onslaught of the sea's waves. Even on sheltered shores the lower limit of salt marsh is normally between MHWN and MHW (Fig. 1.3). Only at very sheltered sites with a small tidal amplitude, e.g. Poole Harbour in Dorset (tidal amplitude 1.1 m), does salt marsh extend below MHWN. Salt marsh will extend as far inland as the sea is able to dominate the ionic content of the soil solution. In the Scheldt Estuary of the S.W. Netherlands, halophytes are replaced by species typical of non-saline soils where the mean salinity of the soil solution drops below $5 \, g \, l^{-1}$ (Beeftink, 1977), a value suggested earlier as a dividing line between salt- and freshwater marsh. It should be stressed that this is only an average and may be modified through inter-action with other environmental variables. The point (with reference to tide height) at which this soil salinity will be reached will depend on drainage of fresh water from the adjacent land into the marsh, concentra-tion of salts by evapotranspiration and the salinity of the inundating water. Where large amounts of fresh water drain into the top of the marsh relative to the input of sea water, the upper limit of the salt marsh may be below HAT or even MHWS. Where there is little input of fresh water combined with a high potential evapotranspiration, as in many of the salt marshes bordering the Mediterranean, a high soil salinity may extend inland well beyond HAT. The salt concentration in the oceans is about $33 \, g \, l^{-1}$. This concentration is changed in some partially enclosed seas according to the balance between freshwater input and evaporative loss. Salinities in the southern Baltic Sea are about $7 \, g \, l^{-1}$ whilst in the eastern Mediterranean Sea they rise to $39 \, g \, l^{-1}$ (*Times World Atlas*, 1980). The higher the average salinity of the adjacent sea water the further inland the saline influence of the sea is likely to extend.

The horizontal width of salt marsh thus depends on tidal amplitude, gradient of the shore and drainage of fresh water into the marsh from the adjacent land mass. Low-lying areas with gently sloping shores exposed to a significant tidal amplitude, such as much of the Atlantic coast of the U.S.A., the Wadden Sea coasts of Holland, Germany and Denmark, and the Essex and Lancashire coasts in England, are particularly suitable for the formation of salt marsh.

1.3 Distribution

The global distribution of salt marshes is illustrated in Fig. 1.4. Towards the poles, salt marsh extends along coasts to the same limits as tundra vegetation, i.e. areas where the temperature of the warmest month exceeds 0°C. Salt marshes are most frequent in the temperate zones, but they are commonly replaced from suitable sites within the tropics by mangroves.

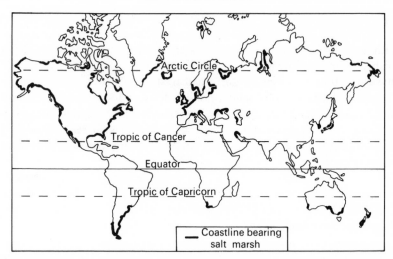

Figure 1.4 World distribution of salt marsh, after Chapman (1977), with additional data from Macdonald (1977) and Jefferies (1977).

Examination of world climate suggests that mangroves replace salt marsh on coasts where the mean temperatures of the coldest and warmest months exceed 10°C and 15.5°C, thus true salt marshes are largely absent from the tropics (Fig. 1.4). However, a type of salt marsh is found on some muddy shores within the tropics where mangrove has failed to develop, and some herbaceous species found on salt marshes outside of the tropics may form a mixed vegetation with mangroves within the tropics (Chapman, 1974a, 1977).

There has been no extensive detailed mapping of the salt marshes of the world and thus accurate figures on the total area occupied by this habitat are not available. Salt marshes are often fragmented, with an irregular shape, and are interspersed with bare drainage channels, so the determination of their area by conventional cartographic techniques is tedious and extremely difficult. The advent of satellite photography combined with computer interpretation of the video images sent back to Earth may soon allow the determination of global salt marsh areas. By analysis of small changes in the visible and infra-red radiation reflected from vegetated surfaces, the area of salt marsh and even the areas occupied by the major plant species may be estimated. The east coast of the U.S.A. alone bears an estimated 600 000 ha of salt marsh. Even a small country such as Britain retains some 40 500 ha, despite extensive reclamation (Reimold, 1977; Nature Conservancy Council, unpublished).

1.4 Types

Within the large total area of salt marsh, different types may be distinguished. A prerequisite for the occurrence of salt marsh is the presence of a physical feature providing protection against the full energy of the waves. A number of different physical features provide such protection and since they are a dominant influence they provide a useful scheme for distinguishing different types of marsh. Six types of marsh may be distinguished: lagoonal, beach plain, barrier island, estuarine, semi-natural and artificial (adapted from Beeftink, 1977).

(1) *Lagoonal marshes* may occur where a sand or shingle spit partially encloses a body of tidal water with only a narrow connection to the sea, thus markedly decreasing both wave energy and tidal amplitude. A good example is Poole Harbour in S. England (Fig. 1.5*A*).

(2) *Beach plains* are either partially protected by sand or shingle bars that are overwashed at high water, or they are unprotected. These are usually narrow marshes formed on otherwise exposed shores and accretion may be affected not only by tidal floodwater, but may also be supplemented by windborne sand. Thus these marshes are often intermediate between salt marsh and sand dune. Wave energy is rarely low enough for salt marsh to form on open coasts, although the 10 km stretch of the Dengie Peninsula marshes to the north of the Thames Estuary (Fig. 1.5*B*) and, on a larger scale, the marshes of the Florida Panhandle, are exceptions (Tanner, 1960; Boorman and Ranwell, 1977).

(3) *Barrier island marshes* occur where a chain of islands provides an offshore barrier, so creating calmer waters in their lee. For example, the extensive salt marshes of the Wadden Sea in W. Europe have formed in the shelter of the Frisian Islands (Fig. 1.5*C*) and similarly the 200 km^2 of salt marsh on the coast of Georgia, U.S.A., have formed in the shelter of a chain of barrier islands which stretch the length of the coast of the state (Beeftink, 1977; Reimold, 1977; Wiegert, 1979).

(4) *Estuarine marshes* may form on sheltered inner curves of estuaries or they may have no physical barrier between themselves and the open sea. However, the shallowness and length of estuaries results in the dissipation of wave energy, allowing the formation of fringing salt marshes. It is probable that every river estuary in the middle and high latitudes contains some area of salt marsh, and thus this type of marsh is probably the most abundant. They are characterized by strong tidal currents and, in contrast to the preceding types, by widely fluctuating salinities in the inundating tidal water (Fig. 1.5*D*).

(5) *Semi-natural marshes* are salt marshes which have been significantly and deliberately modified by man, but still retain some elements of the original saltmarsh community. In New England, drainage ditches have been cut in areas of high marsh to aid mosquito control (Ranwell, 1972). Large areas of high marsh on the southern North Sea coasts have been

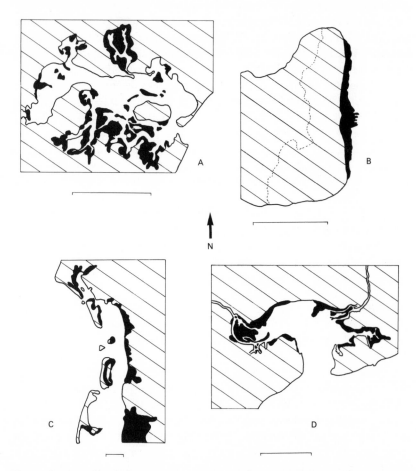

Figure 1.5 Examples of salt marsh types. (A) Poole Harbour, southern England, a lagoonal marsh formed in sheltered water, connected to the English Channel via a narrow inlet. (B) Dengie Peninsula, eastern England, a beach-plain marsh facing the open North Sea; area to the east of the dotted line is reclaimed land. (C) North Wadden Sea, western Denmark, barrier island salt marshes formed in the lee of offshore islands. (D) St. Louis Bay Estuary, Mississippi, U.S.A., an estuarine marsh, formed on the sheltered inner curves. Areas shaded black indicate the extent of salt marsh. The scale bars each represent 5 km.

enclosed by sea walls (Fig. 1.5*B*); however, many still retain a residual saltmarsh flora (Boorman and Ranwell, 1977).

(6) *Artificial marshes* are salt marshes that man has created. The best and most significant examples are areas of spoil dredged from shipping channels in N. America which have been stabilized by planting with the saltmarsh grass *Spartina alterniflora* (Seneca, 1974).

It must be recognized that these types are not mutually exclusive and many marshes exist which are intermediate between the types described above. The next chapter considers the formation of these marshes and the physico-chemical characteristics and variation in this habitat.

CHAPTER TWO

SALTMARSH FORMATION, PHYSIOGRAPHY AND SOILS

Coastal salt marshes are not only biologically unique, but as sites of rapid surface development and change they hold much of interest to the physical geographer. Whilst perceptible changes in the landscapes of dry land may take years, centuries or millennia, a single storm tide may cause noticeable erosion, sediment deposition and alteration of the drainage pattern in a salt marsh. Typically, salt marshes will show a net accretion of sediment with each tide, but some erosion will also occur. The two processes vary differentially in time and space, leading to the formation of a range of permanent and transitory physiographical features, so providing a diversity of biological habitats. This chapter describes the physical processes and biological interactions leading to saltmarsh development and the physicochemical characteristics of the habitat so created.

2.1 Formation

As a broad generalization salt marshes will form according to the following sequence of events (Fig. 2.1). Where sediment accretes on a sheltered shore to above MHWN (see section 1.2 for abbreviation of tidal levels), a few vascular plant species may become established. This vegetation aids continued sedimentation by reducing wave energy, so decreasing scour and binding the sediment. As the surface rises, further plant species invade and the surface becomes fully vegetated, excepting drainage channels and isolated depressions. Accretion of sediment may continue, eventually raising the surface to a height reached only by the highest tides (c. HAT). Completion of this process may take a few years, or centuries, and it will frequently show temporary reversals leading to saltmarsh loss. The rate of saltmarsh formation is determined by the degree of protection that the site is afforded by a protecting coastal feature (p. 9), the topography of the nearshore sea bed and the supply of suspended sediment.

12

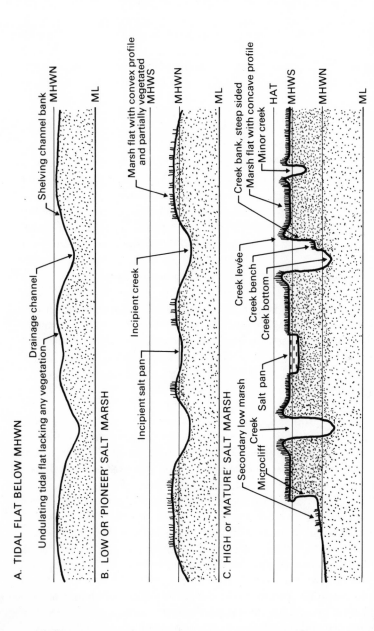

Figure 2.1 Cross-sections of salt marsh and tidal flat illustrating physiographical features and a hypothetical sequence of saltmarsh development, after the descriptions of Beeftink (1966) and Steers (1977), and following the nomenclature of Teal (1962). (A) High level tidal flat. (B) Low level marsh in which vascular plants have colonized the higher points of the tidal flat. (C) High marsh with a fully vegetated surface, except for the creeks and pans which are sharply defined by their steep banks. Secondary low marsh occurs where the surface has been eroded due to creek movement or the formation of an erosion microcliff.

Shelter and topography

If little shelter is afforded, as on many beach plain salt marshes, the marsh will be limited to the area around HAT, since below this level wave energy will be too great to allow either the establishment of vascular plants or the deposition of fine sediment. Conversely, on well sheltered sites, as in many lagoonal salt marshes, the marsh may extend down to MHWN or even below.

Even on well protected shores with a good supply of suspended sediment, topography will have a profound influence on the extent and rate of salt marsh growth. On steeply sloping shores, such as those of the sea lochs of W. Scotland and fjords of S.W. Norway, salt marshes are limited to a few metres in width. On shores dipping along barely perceptible gradients, such as the Mississippi delta in Louisiana and Chesapeake Bay in Maryland and Virginia, salt marshes may extend to several kilometres in width.

Sedimentation

In general, salt marsh forms when sedimentation produces a surface above MHWN, the usual limit for establishment of vascular plants. An exception is where unprotected tidal flats above MHWN are produced by sedimentation, but are too mobile and exposed for the establishment of plants. If a protective feature, such as a sand spit or shingle ridge, subsequently develops seaward of the flats, so providing shelter, then saltmarsh development may commence on the already accreted sediment. Another exception is where freshwater marsh is gradually inundated by sea water on a subsiding coastline, producing the bog-type marshes common in New England (Beeftink, 1977). Here sedimentation is a secondary feature, rather than a precursor of marsh formation. In all cases however, a continued supply of sediment is required for the persistence, growth and development of the marsh.

Sediment may be derived from either the sea bed or the land, according to local conditions. Estuarine marshes and others in the vicinities of large freshwater discharges may derive most of their sediment from the land, e.g. the marshes of the Rhine delta in the south-western Netherlands. Quantities of suspended sediment discharged from rivers may be enormous. The Susquehanna River discharges 50 000–100 000 tonnes of sediment per year into Chesapeake Bay, exceeding the 30 000 tonnes of sediment accreted each year on the 416 km^2 of salt marsh in the bay (Nixon, 1980). Sediment discharged by rivers shows marked variation from day to day. Following periods of exceptionally heavy rain, the sediment discharged by a river in a single day may be more than in an average year (Meadows and Campbell, 1978). Where soft rocks outcrop in the inshore waters, considerable quantities of suspended sediment will be derived from their erosion. For example the sediments of the Bull Island salt marshes in Dublin Bay, Ireland, are derived from Pleistocene drift on the bed of the Irish Sea (Harris, 1977). In addition, windborne silts and sands may be a significant source of sediment, especially in arid climates.

Rates of sedimentation in salt marshes and tidal flats may be measured by a variety of techniques. Distinctive materials such as brick-dust or coloured sands may be sprinkled on to the surface so that depths of sediment subsequently deposited may be determined (Steers, 1964). More recently, use has been made of radioactive products which are incorporated into the sediment, such as ^{210}Pb (produced naturally at a constant rate) or ^{137}Cs (a product of atmospheric nuclear tests) (De Laune and Patrick, 1980; Nixon, 1980). Since these radioactive isotopes have known half-lives, the ages of sediments may be calculated and past sedimentation rates determined. However, the change in height of a surface over a given time interval, even assuming a constant mean sea level, is not simply the thickness of sediment deposited in that interval, since settlement and biological oxidation of the underlying layers will be partially counteracting this increase. Net change in the height of the surface may be measured against marker posts firmly anchored in the underlying substratum. Table 2.1 illustrates annual rates of sedimentation at different levels in four salt marshes. However, annual accretion rates may vary with time. An area of middle marsh dominated by *Spartina patens* in Connecticut has, based on ^{210}Pb measurements, accreted some 24 cm of sediment since 1900, but only 10 cm in the preceding 100 years (McCaffrey, 1977). As might be predicted from variation in sediment supply, amounts of sediment deposited may vary considerably from day to day. Kestner and Inglis (1956) record the deposition of up to 8 mm of sediment following a single spring tide on flats in the Wyre Estuary, N.W. England.

Table 2.1 Accretion rates in four salt marshes ($mm\,y^{-1}$). Data from Chapman (1976) and Patrick and DeLaune (1980).

Marsh level	Scolt Head, E. England	Dovey, Wales	Skallingen, W. Denmark	Barataria Bay, Louisiana
Low	8	78	47	150
Middle	6	42	36	110
High	2	21	13	80

Rates of sedimentation are primarily determined by physical factors, but may be strongly modified by biological and chemical factors. Each tide carries fine mineral particles and organic debris held in suspension by the motion of the water. At the turn of the tide there is a short period with little motion when deposition of this load may occur. In still water, suspended particles will start to fall at an accelerating rate until they reach a terminal velocity (v_0), which may be determined from Stokes' law (eqn. 2.1).

$$v_0 = \frac{2gr^2(\rho - \sigma)}{9\eta} \qquad (2.1)$$

where v_0 is the terminal velocity of the particle (mm s^{-1})
r is the radius of the particle (mm)
g is the acceleration due to gravity (98 mm s^{-2})
η is the viscosity of the water (mg mm^{-1} s^{-1})
ρ is the density of the water (mg mm^{-3})
σ is the density of the particle (mg mm^{-3})

Strictly, this equation applies only to perfect spheres, but will serve as an approximate guide to relative rates of sinking. For example, the settling velocity of a sand particle of radius 0.2 mm and density 2.6 mg mm^{-3} in sea water of density 1.05 mg mm^{-3} would be 1 mm s^{-1}. In other words such a sand particle could settle from a height of 10 cm in just over one and a half minutes. Under the same conditions and assuming the same densities, a particle of radius 0.01 mm, an average size for silt particles, would require one hour to settle out of the same height of water, while individual clay particles ($r < 0.002$ mm) would require many hours or even days to settle.

Since such a small force per surface area is exerted by the settlement of the smallest particles, it will be appreciated that only the slightest water movement would be necessary to keep them in suspension. The result on a shore is that only the largest particles may settle where wave energy is strong or the current is fast, the finer particles only settling in sheltered sites with little current. Similarly, grading will occur as a tide laden with material rises on a shore, the coarse particles settling first so that as the water rises higher up the shore it contains an ever-increasing proportion of smaller particles.

Whilst physical processes govern deposition of sediment, chemical and biological factors may strongly accelerate this process. Individual clay particles will in practice never be able to settle. In pure water, clay particles will remain separate, repelling each other by their negatively charged surfaces. In the presence of electrolytes these charges will be cancelled and the particles may flocculate, i.e. become loosely bound to form larger particles, and thus settle more rapidly. Flocculation will begin in a salinity of about $4\,kg\,m^{-3}$, i.e. just over 10% sea water. In still salt solution, clay particles form a weak gel which sinks, gradually expelling water. This gelling of clay also provides some protection against resuspension. Indeed, once consolidated, clays are less readily eroded than fine sands, despite the smaller size of individual particles (Perkins, 1974a).

The mucous secretions of diatoms bind silt and clay particles, so accelerating their deposition. Holland et al. (1974) showed that addition of mucus-secreting diatoms to agitated flasks of suspended sediment increased the rate of deposition and gave the resulting sediment greater stability. Coles (1979), in a detailed study of the mudflats and salt marshes of the Wash in E. England, concluded that accretion of muds, i.e. clay and silt mixtures, occurred only when mucus produced by the epipelic (i.e. mud and surface dwelling) microflora was present. On intertidal flats in the temperate zone the most important group of this microflora are the epipelic diatoms. In the Wash, densities of epipelic diatoms in the upper $1.5\,mm$ of sediment ranged from $1000\,cm^{-2}$ in exposed sand flats to $550\,000\,cm^{-2}$ in the salt marsh. Other algae may decrease the erodibility of fresh sediment by forming a surface mat. *Phormidium* spp. may re-establish such a surface mat within 24 hours of being buried in $4\,mm$ of fresh sediment. Macroalgae may also help to stabilize sediment. Sediment covered by *Enteromorpha*, a common species within and just seaward of salt marsh, is not eroded by water moving at velocities of up to five times those needed to erode the same surface in the absence of the alga (Scoffin, 1970).

Invertebrate feeders may destabilize an accreting surface. For example, *Hydrobia* and *Corophium* will graze epipelic diatoms, whilst deposit feeders may re-work the sediment, loosening it and so making it more susceptible to erosion. Letzsch and Frey (1980), at Sapelo Island in Georgia, showed that decapods excavated 20% of the saltmarsh creek surfaces within a single year.

Upward growth of the marsh surface

Once the combined physicochemical and biological processes have stabilized intertidal flats and raised them to above MHWN, vascular plant colonization may begin. The small hummocks or raised areas sometimes found around the bases of isolated plants or clumps of vegetation on the lowest levels of the marsh (e.g. Fig. 2.2) are clear evidence that the vascular

Figure 2.2 Pioneer growth of *Spartina anglica* at the level reached by the high water of neap tides on mudflats of the River Colne Estuary, E. England. The raised surface around this growth suggests that the presence of this pioneer vegetation has either enhanced accretion or inhibited erosion of the surface.

plant vegetation either assists accretion of the surface or decreases its erodibility. Vascular plants may assist the deposition of further material in four ways. Their roots and rhizome systems help to bind the sediment, while shoots locally decrease flow and wave energy, so encouraging sedimentation. They add organic matter to the sediment by their growth, and appear to deter filter feeding invertebrates which might otherwise rework the sediment. For example, *Spartina* spp. in many parts of the world are among the first vascular plants to invade bare tidal flats suitable for saltmarsh formation. They will produce a fine surface root mat in the upper 2–3 cm, which protects the sediment surface, together with a system of large anchoring roots, penetrating down 1–2 m and helping to stabilize the sediment. Shoots of *S. alterniflora* at the seaward edge of salt marshes in the south-eastern U.S.A. may reach heights of 2–3 m and densities of about $800 \, \text{m}^{-2}$. This forest of shoots would clearly represent a significant frictional drag to currents in the rising and falling tide, protecting the marsh surface against erosion and encouraging sedimentation by promoting still conditions. Frey and Basan (1978) report mature *S. alterniflora* reducing the height of wind-generated waves by 71 % and wave energy by

92%. Production of roots and rhizomes may amount to $1–3\,kg\,m^{-2}\,y^{-1}$ (Chapter 5) which, by directly adding volume to the sediment could, assuming an 85% water content, raise the surface by between 0.7–$2.0\,cm\,y^{-1}$. The incorporation into the sediment of shoot litter must also be added, though this gain will be reduced by decomposition. In some marshes, plant matter accumulation in the sediment is clearly the major method by which continued growth occurs, since saltmarsh peats are formed.

In the earliest stages of plant colonization, saltmarsh growth is irregular, since sediment deposited by one tide may be washed away by the next. As the vegetation becomes established, conditions become more stable. If there is good plant cover to retain deposited sediment, then sedimentation should be greatest in the lowest parts of the marsh, since these are covered most frequently and for the longest periods. In general, the rate of sedimentation appears to decrease inversely with elevation, as illustrated for a range of marshes in Table 2.1. However, Ranwell (1972) reported maximum rates of accretion occurring in the middle levels of a salt marsh at Bridgwater Bay.

Continued accretion means, in theory, that an area of low salt marsh will eventually be transformed into high marsh reached only by the highest tides. Such changes in level will be accompanied by successional changes in the flora and fauna (Chapters 3, 4). In practice, however, coastal features are rarely stable and such a sequence of marsh building may often be interrupted or even reversed. For example, drainage channels in estuaries may show periodic shifts, so altering the currents to which the marsh edges are subjected. Gray (1972), in a study of Morecambe Bay, N.W. England, showed, from past maps, a correspondence between periodic building and erosion of salt marsh and changes in the position of the River Kent drainage channel. Shingle ridges protecting salt marshes may be breached by storms, so exposing the marsh to erosion. Similarly, storms may force shingle ridges landward over the marsh surface, so smothering the vegetation and then exposing the denuded surface to the open sea (Butler et al., 1981; Greensmith and Tucker, 1966).

2.2　Physiographic features

The upward growth of a salt marsh is accompanied by the development of distinct physiographic features. From a distance, large coastal salt marshes may appear as uninteresting expanses of remarkably flat land dominated

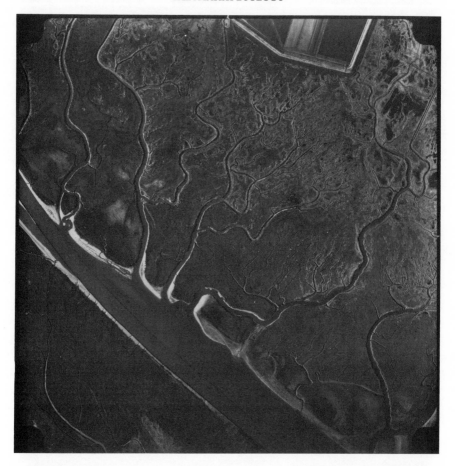

Figure 2.3 Vertical aerial view of salt marsh on the Wash, E. England. The marsh surface is fragmented by a highly divided system of creeks and dotted with salt pans. Areas of lighter shade surrounding the creeks of the upper right quarter of the plate indicate a difference in the vegetation associated with the well drained and raised creek levees by comparison to the poorly drained areas, between the creeks, which are of a darker shade. (Photo: Aerial Photography Unit, Cambridge University: copyright reserved.)

by grass or low shrubs. Close up, or viewed from the air (Fig. 2.3), a very different picture is obtained. The surface is intricately dissected by a dense network of drainage creeks, often dotted with small pools or salt pans, and may include small cliffs or ridges.

Creeks

The tidal drainage channels, termed creeks, are arguably the most distinctive feature of the mature salt marsh. In aerial view they may be seen to ramify throughout the marsh, dividing and meandering to form complex patterns. At Colne Point salt marsh in E. England, the detailed mapping of a hectare of salt marsh, distant from the main drainage creek, showed that minor creeks occupied 26% of the total area and included over 1 km of creek bank (Hussey and Long, 1982). In cross-section, creeks are typically steep-sided, dropping from the marsh surface to a bed typically at or below MHWN. The banks may include step-like benches at varying heights and the tops typically show a surface raised above the surrounding marsh and termed a levee (Fig. 2.1).

Steers (1977) suggests that in the salt marshes of Scolt Head in Norfolk, E. England, creeks originate during marsh inception. Pioneer plants spread from patches which form first on sheltered and often high points of the original bare flat. Their lateral growth concentrates the flow of the water into definite channels, the bottoms of which mark approximately the level of the original surface (Fig. 2.4). However, on other marshes, e.g. Bull

Figure 2.4   A young creek in low level marsh on mudflats of the River Colne Estuary, E. England, recently colonized (*c.* 10–30 yrs.) by *Spartina anglica.* The creek walls are shallow and convex (see also Fig. 2.1*B*).

Figure 2.5   A creek in the middle levels of well established marsh (> 400 yrs.) at Colne Point, E. England, during high water of a neap tide (see also Fig. 2.1C). Note the steep sides characteristic of creeks in middle and high marsh formed on fine textured substrates (cf. Fig. 2.4). Although the saltmarsh flat is dominated by the grass *Puccinellia maritima*, dense growths of *Halimione portulacoides* fringe the creek and *Aster tripolium* with *Suaeda maritima* occupy the lower level of the creek bench which fronts the promontory in the centre of the picture.

Island near Dublin in Eire (Harris, 1977) and Dengie Peninsula in Essex (Boorman and Ranwell, 1977), distinct channels resembling creeks may be seen in the tidal flats seaward of the salt marsh. These would be expected to be precursors of the major creeks of the salt marsh. Pestrong (1965) suggested that such channels seaward of the San Francisco Bay salt marshes actually eroded back into the marsh, creating creeks. Once formed, creeks are maintained by the continual scour of the flood and ebb of the tides. Vegetation will spread to the tops of the creek banks, and sometimes part of the way down the walls, so stabilizing the position of the creeks in the marsh (Fig. 2.5). The vegetation promotes accretion on the tops, whilst tidal scour simultaneously maintains or deepens the creek bottom, producing a steep-sided channel (Fig. 2.1C).

Although creek courses may appear to resemble river courses close to sea level in their meandering patterns (Fig. 2.3), they differ hydrologically in two important aspects. First, flow is in two directions, up-channel against the slope of the bed during the flood and down-channel during the ebb. The ebb flow usually reaches the greatest velocities since it is aided by gravity. Secondly, in middle marsh at MHW, creeks reach the bankful condition roughly 360 times in a year, compared to once in every two to three years in many rivers (Leeks, 1979). As most changes in channel form occur during the bankful condition, changes in creek form are far more rapid than in rivers. Indeed, maps of the San Francisco Bay marshes from 1853–1965 show shifts of more than 100 m in the position of the major drainage creeks, marked changes in creek width and capture of one tributary creek by another at a number of locations (Pestrong, 1965). Letzsch and Frey (1980), at Sapelo Island in Georgia, U.S.A., measured rates of creek slope retreat ranging from 68 cm y^{-1} in the most stable areas to 444 cm y^{-1} in the least stable areas. The length and shape of a creek can change continually. As water leaves the marsh flat with the ebb tide, miniature waterfalls arise on the creek banks and head, so cutting new tributary creeks and lengthening the creek by headward erosion (Steers, 1977). Where creek banks are eroded by flow within the channel, undercutting of the more resistant upper layer bound by plant roots can occur (Fig. 2.6). Eventually this will lead to slumping of the vegetated top (Pestrong, 1965). Secondary marsh may develop on the slumped blocks, which may form a bench in the creek bank (Fig. 2.1C). Sometimes a collapse will dam a creek, and if vegetation becomes well established the

Figure 2.6   Slumping of the creek bank as a result of undercutting is often seen in the middle and upper salt marsh.

blockage may become permanent, so creating an isolated pool or channel pan and shortening the creek.

Creek systems appear to vary in complexity according to the substrate on which the marsh has formed. Where marsh sediments have a high clay or silt content, as in the salt marshes of E. England, or a high peat content, as in many marshes of the eastern U.S.A., very intricate dendritic drainage systems are found. Where sediments have a high sand content, such as the salt marshes of W. Denmark, Ireland and W. England, creek densities are lower and creeks show less branching (Chapman, 1977). Presumably this difference results from the better surface drainage in sandy sediments, so decreasing or preventing erosion and extension through surface run-off during the ebb. As a biological habitat, creeks provide over a short distance (often of less than 1 m) a gradient from MHWN or below up to the level of the marsh flat, which could be viewed as a microcosm of the gradient over the salt marsh as a whole. For creeks in the middle levels of the marsh, the levees are often sufficiently raised above the adjacent marsh flat to allow invasion by species more typical of the upper marsh, whilst benches in the creek, which form below the level of the marsh flat, may be colonized by species typical of the lower marsh. Since tidal waters enter and leave the marsh via the creeks, exchange of materials between the marsh and the inundating waters will be most rapid on the creek banks. Thus the creeks will be the sites which reflect most closely the chemical composition of the tidal waters and will be the least prone both to hyper-salination through evaporative concentration of salt and to stagnation of soil water. However, it is also the part of the marsh which is subjected to the greatest degree of scour by the tides and this no doubt explains the lack of vascular plant vegetation on many creek walls.

Salt pans

Salt pans are depressions in the marsh surface which are largely devoid of vascular plant vegetation. They vary in size from a few square metres up to five hundred square metres (Butler *et al.*, 1981). Following heavy rains or spring tides they will retain standing water for many days, whilst in dry spells coincident with neap tides, the pans may dry out leaving a surface layer of crystalline salt (Fig. 2.7).

Pans are believed to originate in a number of ways. Primary coloniza-tion of the marsh surface is uneven and results in the enclosure of some bare areas, usually at the sites of slight depressions in the original surface. When this happens water can no longer escape after a flooding tide, and

Figure 2.7   Salt pans, seen here on the middle salt marsh of the St. Osyth Marshes in E. England, are shallow unvegetated depressions in the marsh surface which hold water following spring tides or rain (see also Fig. 2.1*C*).

plant colonization is discouraged either by waterlogging or by hyper-salination during dry periods. Once formed, pans usually have well defined margins, produced and maintained by the miniature waves which are generated in them during strong winds and by the swirl of water entering the pan during the rise of a spring or storm tide (Steers, 1977). Pans formed during salt marsh initiation are termed "primary pans". Where creeks cut back into pans providing drainage, vascular plants will colonize the floor of the old pan. Thus as a marsh ages a decrease in pan density might be expected. However, Pethick (1974) and Butler *et al.* (1981) have shown in marshes in E. England that pan density increases with height and presumably the age of the marsh surface. Part of this increase may be explained by the creation of channel pans (p. 23), but these may be identified by their typically ribbon-like shape and do not account for all of the increase. Some other mechanism causing pan formation must therefore be operating. Rafts of tidal litter deposited on the marsh may smother patches of vegetation leading to so-called "rotten spots". Yapp *et al.* (1917) hypothesized that erosion of these denuded surfaces would result in pan formation. Ranwell (1972) reported incipient pan formation following the development of "rotten spots" on a salt marsh at Bridgwater Bay, S.W. England.

However, Reidenbaugh and Banta (1980) found no evidence of pan formation following the development of "rotten spots" on a Virginia salt marsh dominated by *Spartina alterniflora*. The "rotten spots" in this case were eventually recolonized by vascular plants. Butler *et al.* (1981) suggest that pans may form where surface run-off creates small tributary creeks at right angles to an existing creek. As water rises in the larger creek on the flood an eddy will be created in the small creek, producing a keyhole shape, i.e. a circular head with a narrow connection to the main creek. If the banks of the connection slump and create a dam, the circular head will then be isolated, creating a pan. Butler *et al.* (1981) report several examples of pans adjacent to creeks which show evidence of a previous narrow connection to the creek. Jefferies *et al.* (1979*b*) report the formation of pans in the upper marsh at La Pérouse on Hudson Bay by the removal of patches of turf by grazing snow geese.

As a habitat salt pans provide many contrasts to creeks. In many respects pans may be viewed as the saltmarsh equivalent of rock pools on rocky shores, trapping some of the same animals and algae. On middle and high salt marsh, days or even months may elapse between tidal inundations. Salinities may thus vary considerably from that of the tidal water, depending on the prevailing weather. The stagnant water and permanent waterlogging result in a highly anaerobic soil. Even if the surface dries in the summer months it will usually form a hard salt-saturated crust overlying an anaerobic soil at 1–2 cm. The highly anaerobic conditions combined with occasional hypersalination probably explain the absence of vascular plants. However, the standing water provides an aquatic habitat within the marsh for marine algae and fauna, which, unlike the creeks, is not subjected to the twice daily scour of the tides.

Saltmarsh cliff

Where tidal conditions change such that erosion of material exceeds deposition, a microcliff may form, eroding the mature saltmarsh surface as it retreats landward. Typically these cliffs range from 10–100 cm in height, depending on tidal amplitude and the height of the marsh surface relative to mean sea level. Erosion undercuts the mature marsh surface which slumps. The slumped surface is then washed away, leaving a clean cliff face (Fig. 2.8). The eroded lower level surface which results may then be colonized by pioneer species, creating new low-level secondary marsh. Greensmith and Tucker (1966) describe a cycle of saltmarsh erosion and cliff formation, followed by a period of deposition of fresh sediment in front of

Figure 2.8   A salt marsh cliff, about 1 m high, formed by erosion of middle salt marsh on the River Colne Estuary, E. England. Wave action has undercut the marsh surface causing slumping. The slumped blocks are subsequently eroded, so converting the marsh to bare mudflat.

the microcliff, at Dengie Peninsula in Essex, E. England. The cutting faces of saltmarsh cliffs are invariably devoid of vegetation, but often provide a clear profile of the past depositional history of the marsh and its soil.

Saltmarsh flat

The saltmarsh flat is the main vegetated surface at all levels of the marsh and will typically constitute upwards of 70% of the total surface area. Saltmarsh levels are classified according to the level of this flat. The lowest third of this altitudinal range constitutes the lower marsh, the middle third the middle marsh and the highest third the upper marsh. Typically the saltmarsh flat will rise gently from the adjacent tidal flats to its landward limit (Fig. 1.3). Across this gradient a number of gradual changes may be perceived (Beeftink, 1966). First, in the low marsh the flat tends to show a convex cross-section dipping towards the creeks, whilst in the high marsh the development of levees gives the flat a concave cross-section rising towards the creeks (Fig. 2.1). Secondly, a general levelling of the flat occurs at the higher levels since, as the marsh develops, lower areas will trap more sediment, so effectively allowing them to catch up with the adjacent higher areas. Thirdly, the marsh flat becomes increasingly dissected in the middle and upper marsh, with the development of small tributary creeks.

The gradual rise in level across the marsh provides a gradient of decreasing tidal influence. For example, at Poole Harbour, in S. England, marsh at MHWN will be covered by more than 700 tides per annum, amounting to 3600 hours of submergence in a year compared to 50 tides and just 400 hours of submergence for marsh at MHWS (calculated from Ranwell, 1972; Admiralty, 1980).

Middle and high marsh flat, away from creeks and pans, appears

Figure 2.9   Zonation of vegetation in relation to slight changes in elevation and substrate on the middle levels of salt marsh at Colne Point, E. England. Tall shrubs of *Suaeda fruticosa* (= *S. vera*) occupy the higher and better drained ground to the right. This gives way to the lower shrubby growths of *Halimione portulacoides* in the centre and a community dominated by the grass *Puccinellia maritima* in the lowest and least well drained ground on the left.

remarkably level and may vary less than a few centimetres in height over hundreds of metres in distance. However, even small changes in height result in significant changes in the habitat. Boorman (1971), using a micro-topograph to detect small height changes, has shown how local changes in the vegetation can be related to height changes on the marsh of only a few centimetres. A small hump in the surface of only 2–3 cm will be reached by significantly fewer tides and, since it is raised above the adjacent flat, will drain more readily. Very obvious differences in the composition of vegetation are seen with larger changes in the surface level (e.g. Fig. 2.9).

2.3   Sea level change

The theoretical pattern of saltmarsh growth described earlier (section 2.1) assumes a constant sea level relative to the land. Coastlines are rarely stable since it is probable that most coasts outside of the tropics are rising or falling relative to sea level. Glaciation resulted in a transfer of weight from the oceans to the glaciated land mass. This change in weight distribution deformed the earth's crust (Bloom, 1967). The removal of this weight from the previously glaciated land mass initiated compensatory isostatic movements of the earth's crust, which continue to the present. In general, areas that bore a great thickness of ice during the last glaciation are slowly rising, whilst areas outside the glaciated zone are showing a compensatory sinking. Thus, in Britain, S.E. England, which was not glaciated, is sinking relative to sea level whilst N.W. Scotland is rising (Steers, 1977).

On rising coastlines there is typically a narrow belt of marsh, e.g. southern Scandinavia and much of the Pacific coast of N. America (Chapman, 1977; Macdonald, 1977). Exceptions to this pattern occur where the adjacent sea is very shallow so that large areas of bed become exposed as a result of a small uplift. The very extensive salt marshes present today in James Bay in N. Canada, and much of the Skallingen salt marsh in W. Denmark, have arisen largely within this century as a result of the uplifting of very shallow sea beds (Glooschenko, 1978; Meesenburg, 1971). On such coastlines the upper levels of the salt marsh are gradually raised, by the general uplift of the land, above the height reached by the highest tides, so limiting the extent of salt marsh.

In contrast, the Atlantic coast of N. America and the North Sea coasts of S.E. England and the Netherlands are sinking relative to sea level. Carbon dating of peat deposits and examination of ^{210}Pb contents of saltmarsh profiles have suggested a sinking of about 3 mm y^{-1} for the Atlantic coast of the U.S.A. and very similar maximum rates for the Essex coast (Butler,

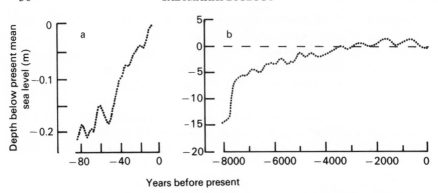

Figure 2.10   Changes in mean sea level (a) at New York City, U.S.A., over the past 80 years, based on tide gauge records (after Nixon, 1980), and (b) in N.W. England over the past 8000 years, extrapolated from radiocarbon dating (after Tooley, 1975).

1978; Nixon, 1980). Here saltmarsh building may be counteracted by sinking of the land surface so that there is no net change in height. On such a coastline, thicknesses of saltmarsh sediment many metres in depth may accumulate.

Rates of sinking or uplifting are not constant (Fig. 2.10). On the Essex coast, as on the Atlantic coast of N. America, sea level has risen progressively over the past 10 000 years, but with some relatively minor oscillations or stillstands. At times of stillstands in sea level the saltmarsh surface may build above MHWS and become dried and consolidated. On recommencement of sea level rise, the old desiccated marsh surface may be buried by new soft sediment and so the process is repeated, leaving a record of previous sea level. These layers in some Essex marshes have been carbon dated and show that up to 30 m of deposit may have accumulated in the past 10 000 years (Leeks, 1979). During periods of rapid sinking the successional changes in the saltmarsh vegetation seen during marsh building may be reversed so that middle marsh becomes low marsh or reverts to bare mud flat.

2.4   Soil

Saltmarsh soils share features with natural inland saline soils, or solonchaks; both are usually poorly draining, show surface salt crystallization and the development of a hard crust on drying. Coastal saltmarsh soils also show parallels to river alluvial soils: both are formed by deposition of waterborne sediment, contain a good supply of many nutrients and have a high cation exchange capacity.

As a result of the processes leading to saltmarsh formation, outlined earlier, the soil invariably contains a larger proportion of clay and silt particles than the marine or intertidal sediments underlying the marsh, which were deposited before saltmarsh inception. For example, the salt-marsh soil at Talsarnau in W. Wales is a mud overlying a sand base (Steers, 1977) whilst at Colne Point in E. England a soil rich in clay and silt overlies a gravel base (Butler *et al.*, 1981). On recently subsided coastlines the base may be the preceding terrestrial surface. For example, some salt marshes of the Bay of Fundy, W. Canada, overlie remains of beech and pine forests (Chapman, 1976).

Mineral and organic composition

Mineral composition varies from very sandy soils, through silts to pre-dominantly clay. For example, saltmarsh soil at Bull Island in Dublin Bay, Ireland, contains about 75% sand compared to 5% at Colne Point, E. England (Harris, 1977; Butler, 1978). A soil survey of *Spartina alterniflora* marshes in N. Carolina showed sand contents ranging from 47% to 97% (Broome *et al.*, 1975a). Similar ranges of variation may be found in the organic contents of saltmarsh soils. The surface 4 cm of a Delaware *Spartina alterniflora* marsh contained, as a proportion of total dry weight, roughly 50% organic matter compared to 8% for a *Puccinellia maritima*-dominated salt marsh in Morecambe Bay, N.W. England (Gray and Bunce, 1972; Nixon, 1980). The relative proportions of sand, silt, clay and peat will determine the pore space of the soil. Pore space in peats ranges from 75–90% and in clays from 50–65% (Chapman, 1976). Sandy soils have the lowest pore space but also the lowest resistance to water move-ment because they have a lower proportion of colloids and imbibing surfaces than clays and peats.

Organic content will often show an increase with marsh elevation. For example, at Cefni, N. Wales, organic content ranged from *c.* 8% in the lowest levels of the marsh to *c.* 13% and *c.* 25% in the middle and high marsh respectively, although considerable variation existed at all levels (calculated from Packham and Liddle, 1970). The organic matter is derived from two sources. First, plants which grow on the marsh provide shoot litter which may be incorporated into the soil surface, whilst death of roots and rhizomes adds organic matter to the soil at varying depths. Secondly, particulate organic matter derived from coastal waters is trapped into the soil by sediment accretion (Nixon, 1980).

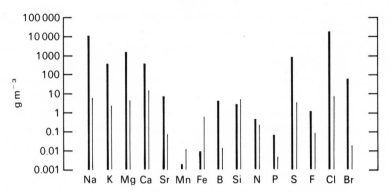

Figure 2.11   Elemental composition of sea water (thick bars) compared to the means for a range of inland waters (thin bars). After Goldberg (1963) and Livingstone (1963).

Ionic content

The inorganic composition of sea water (Fig. 2.11) is the predominant influence on the ionic composition of the soil water of the lower and middle levels of the marsh, extending its influence into the higher levels during dry weather following spring tides. The significance of tidal inundation may be appreciated when sea water is compared with terrestrial river water. Sea water has roughly one thousand times the inorganic solute concentration and a different proportion of ions. The predominant ions, in order of concentration, are Cl^-, Na^+, SO_4^{2-}, and Mg^{2+}, whilst in rivers HCO_3^-, Ca^{2+}, SO_4^{2-} and Cl^- are most likely to head the list. In examining salinity tolerance, attention has focused on the two most abundant ions, Na^+ and Cl^-, but many other ions are elevated well above levels experienced in non-saline soils. Mg^{2+} is present at 500 times its typical concentration in rivers and Br^-, usually present as a trace in rivers, is found at concentrations of $65\,g\,m^{-3}$.

Although the flooding sea water is the dominant influence, the ionic content of the soil will be modified by climate and biological activity. Rainfall will leach the salts downwards and evapotranspiration will concentrate the salts. The mechanical composition of the soil will determine how rapidly flooding sea water or rain water can penetrate the soil. Clay and organic matter provide ion exchange sites which will buffer the soil against salinity fluctuations and cause greater retention of salts. Finally, some vascular plant species extract salt from lower levels of the soil and then excrete the salt through their shoots and on to the soil surface.

It is not simply Na and Cl which are elevated in saltmarsh soils. By

Table 2.2 Ranges for specific concentrations of the major cations $(mg\,kg^{-1})$ and average mechanical composition of dried samples of soils in three salt marshes compared to the normal range for inland soils.

Ion	(1) Morecambe Bay, N.W. England	(2) Cefni, Wales	(3) Colne Point, E. England	(4) "Inland soils"
Na	25–15 500	700–23 000	4800–44 000	13–550
K	13–1200	100–1300	200–4000	11–100
Mg	46–3500	50–3100	400–4200	21–250
Ca	1200–49 300	60–3600	400–3100	550–2000
% Organic	8.4	13.0	22.0	
% Silt	12.0	44.0	32.0	
% Clay	8.0	16.0	41.0	

Calculated from (1) Gray and Bunce (1972), (2) Packham and Liddle (1970), (3) Othman (1980) and (4) Bidwell (1979).

comparison to the range typical of inland soils, K, Mg and Ca are all very high (Table 2.2). The consistently higher values of these ions recorded for the soil at Colne Point correspond to a higher clay and organic content, which would be expected to provide a higher cation exchange capacity.

Reduced saltmarsh soils have been shown to act as sinks for heavy metals, holding significant quantities of Zn, Fe and Mn (Elderfield and Hepworth, 1975). Table 2.3 compares two sites in S.W. Wales. Salthouse Bridge on the Burry Inlet is distant from any immediate industrial source of heavy metals, while the Lower Tawe Estuary in Swansea receives drainage from smelter slag heaps. By comparison to the ranges for unpolluted inland soils, the saltmarsh soil shows exceptionally high Fe and Zn contents. Coastal pollution can raise these levels markedly, as demonstrated by the comparison with the Lower Tawe where levels of Pb, Zn and Cu are roughly ten times greater than at Salthouse Bridge. A rise in Pb levels in a Massachusetts salt marsh from $4\,mg\,kg^{-1}$ to $120\,mg\,kg^{-1}$ in the

Table 2.3 Trace metal concentrations $(mg\,kg^{-1})$ in dried soil samples from lower salt marsh at two locations in S.W. Wales (after Kay and Rajanvipart, 1977) compared with normal ranges for inland soils (after Bidwell, 1979).

Location	Depth	Cu	Fe	Mn	Ni	Pb	Zn
Salthouse	0–2 cm	14	22 900	536	10	23	95
Point	13–15 cm	13	21 700	713	8	19	88
Lower Tawe	0–2 cm	229	63 400	804	72	174	914
(Swansea)	13–15 cm	201	48 000	601	70	131	601
Inland soils		10–1000	1–525	1–4000	—	—	3–20

Table 2.4 Extractable phosphorus contents of saltmarsh soils, expressed as proportion of total dry weight ($mg\,kg^{-1}$).

Location	Max.	Mean	Min.	Source
Morecambe Bay, N.W. England	82	27	5	Gray and Bunce (1972)
Colne Point, E. England	33	12	2	Othman (1980)
Block Island Sound, Rhode Island, U.S.A.	28	20	12	Nixon (1980)
Barataria Bay, Louisiana, U.S.A.	148	123	48	Nixon (1980)
Several freshwater marshes, U.S.A.	7520	1985	46	Nixon (1980)
Inland soils, normal range	5000	—	50	Bidwell (1979)

surface layers of the soil has been correlated with increased atmospheric pollution from traffic on a local freeway (Nixon, 1980).

While sea water provides a rich supply of the major metal ions essential to living organisms, i.e. K, Mg, and Ca, the two most important non-metal nutrients, nitrogen and phosphorus, occur at concentrations 3–4 orders of magnitude lower (Fig. 2.11). Reported levels of extractable P in saltmarsh soils are low compared to inland marshes and at the lower end of the range suggested for inland soils (Table 2.4). Considerable seasonal variation in the levels of extractable P may occur. Othman (1980) found that P contents of the upper 5 cm of salt marsh soil at Colne Point varied from $30\,mg\,kg^{-1}$ in the early summer to $4\,mg\,kg^{-1}$ by the late autumn. Contents also decrease with depth. Total P in a Louisiana *Spartina alterniflora* marsh decreased from $650\,mg\,kg^{-1}$ at 2 cm to $450\,mg\,kg^{-1}$ at 20 cm. Although pure sea water can supply little dissolved P (Fig. 2.11), suspended sediment in coastal waters may constitute a very significant source. Both marine and freshwater sediments appear to contain more P than salt-marsh soil. Thus regardless of source, sediment accreted on to the marsh should elevate soil P (Nixon, 1980). Suspended sediment in coastal waters may have a P content of about $500\,mg\,kg^{-1}$, so that even a modest accretion rate of $1\,mm\,yr^{-1}$ would contribute $1.3\,g\,m^{-2}$. This would explain both the higher levels of P reported in the Barataria Bay marshes (Table 2.4), where sediment accretion is unusually high at about $10\,mm\,y^{-1}$, and the summer peak of P, reported by Othman (1980) at Colne Point which corresponds to the period of maximum sediment accretion. Phosphorus inputs can be considerably elevated by coastal pollution. Beeftink *et al.* (1977) found a linear decline seaward in the P levels associated with the clay fractions of saltmarsh soils along the polluted Scheldt estuary in the S.W. Netherlands.

Salt marshes also derive significant quantities of nitrogen from accreted sediment, the bulk of this being organically bound N. Nitrogen-fixing bacteria and blue-green algae will add N to the soil. In a salt marsh on the Atlantic coast of Nova Scotia, 20% of nitrogenase activity (N_2-fixation capacity), as determined by the acetylene reduction assay, was associated with the surface algae and the bulk of the remainder with the bacteria associated with plant roots (Mann, 1979). Both free-living and infective nitrogen fixing bacteria have been isolated from the rhizosphere and the cortical root cells, respectively, of *S. alterniflora* (Patriquin, 1978; Mann, 1979). Other saltmarsh vascular plants may also show symbiotic relationships with nitrogen-fixing bacteria (Patriquin, 1978). However, this gain will be, to some extent, counteracted by populations of denitrifying bacteria (Kaplan *et al.*, 1977; Sherr and Payne, 1978). Nixon (1980), in reviewing the information available for the east coast marshes of the U.S.A., concluded that the net result of these two processes would be a loss to the salt marsh of about $5-10 \, g(N) \, m^{-2} \, y^{-1}$. Similarly, a net loss of $2.5 \, g(N) \, m^{-2} \, y^{-1}$ can be calculated for salt marsh in E. England (estimated from Aziz and Nedwell, 1979; Aziz, 1979). Nitrogen in saltmarsh soil is predominantly in the organic form which slowly decomposes to yield inorganic forms (Chapter 6). Organic-N, averaged from monthly measurements over two years at Colne Point in E. England, amounted to $968.8 \, mg \, kg^{-1}$, compared to $17.1 \, mg \, kg^{-1}$ for NH_4-N and $2.5 \, mg \, kg^{-1}$ for NO_3-N and NO_2-N, combined (Aziz, 1979). However, the inorganic forms show considerable seasonal fluctuations. Henriksen and Jensen (1979) at Skallingen, W. Denmark, observed a spring peak concentration of 3.0 mM in the amounts of combined free and exchangeable inorganic forms of N. which declined to 0.1 mM in the late summer (Table 2.5). Concentrations

Table 2.5 Combined concentrations of exchangeable and free inorganic nitrogen in the soil solution of the middle salt marsh at two locations (Abd. Aziz, 1979; Henriksen and Jensen, 1979) compared to concentrations suggested for hydroponic culture (Bidwell, 1979). Values (mM) were recorded in May, with August values in parenthesis.

N-form	Colne Point, E. England	Skallingen, W. Denmark	Concentration for hydroponic culture
NH_4^+	1.4 (0.60)	1.7 (0.07)	—
NO_3^-/NO_2^-	0.5 (0.02)	1.2 (0.03)	10.0

of inorganic nitrogen recommended for hydroponic culture of crop plants are 10 mM (Bidwell, 1979) or 100 times the available levels observed in the late summer in the soils of the Skallingen marshes. The fact that these levels of available nitrogen are strongly limiting to the growth of saltmarsh vascular plants *in situ* is demonstrated by the sharp increase in dry matter yields which follows the addition of nitrogen fertilizers (Valiela and Teal, 1974). This topic is dealt with in further detail in Chapter 5.

Water and waterlogging

Water alternately floods and drains from the saltmarsh soil causing a cyclical rise and fall in the water table. The ease with which this water gains access to and drains from the soil depends on the soil structure and topography of the marsh. At low tide, water seeps laterally into the empty creeks and continues to do so until water starts to flood into the creeks again. As the creek fills, water is forced out laterally, first through the lower strata or sub-soil and eventually through the upper layers of the soil. If the tide overtops the creeks, the soil surface will also be flooded and water will percolate downwards. As the tide ebbs, the surface water will run off the flat into the creeks, leaving pools in any depressions. As the level drops in the creeks the lateral flow out of the creeks will be reversed and drainage will recommence, completing the cycle. Not all tides will flood the marsh flat, indeed on the highest parts of the marsh only storm or equinoctial tides will do so. When tides do not rise above the creek levees (e.g. Fig. 2.5), input and drainage of sea water at any one point on the marsh flat will depend on the permeability of the soil and the distance from a creek.

The high clay, silt and organic matter contents, repeated flooding, and the flatness of the marsh surface result in frequent or almost continuous waterlogging. Waterlogging is a permanent feature of the low marsh and, where drainage is impeded, it is common in the middle and high marsh. Salinity promotes waterlogging by lowering the water vapour pressure, so depressing evaporation, and by affecting the organization of clay particles so that a largely structureless soil with a low hydraulic conductivity is produced.

Armstrong (1976) provides a detailed account of the effects of water-logging on soils. The basic effect of waterlogging in the salt marsh, as in other soils, is that oxygen supply is limited and the soil will become anaerobic. Under these conditions microbial populations develop which make use of electron acceptors other than oxygen for their respiratory oxidations. This results in the conversion of numerous compounds into a chemically reduced state which is reflected in a lowering of the oxidation–reduction potential, or redox, of the whole soil. Redox is commonly measured as the potential difference generated between a hydrogen and a platinum electrode across the soil at pH 7.0. Redox (E_7) ranges from 250 mV upwards for soils containing detectable oxygen, down to − 500 mV or below for highly reduced anaerobic soils. Redox at 2 cm depth in the salt marsh at Colne Point ranged from + 50 mV to + 100 mV on the saltmarsh flat, − 100 mV to − 150 mV in the creek bottoms and − 250 mV to − 350 mV in salt pans (Aziz, 1979). Redox typically decreases with depth, as illustrated in a salt marsh in Mission Bay, California, where E_7 was + 200 mV on the surface of the low marsh flat, − 20 mV at 0.5 cm, and − 145 mV at 12 cm (Bradshaw, 1968).

The reducing potential within these soils is provided by both inorganic and organic compounds. Ions of most transition elements will approach their most reduced states at any depth in the sediment. At redox values of + 200 mV the large quantities of Mn in saltmarsh soils (p. 33) will be predominantly in the divalent state, and similarly at E_7 of + 100 mV and below iron will be predominantly present as free divalent ferrous ion. A common and more obvious feature of the reduced nature of the soil is the grey or black coloration seen when the surface few mm are removed. This is a result of the precipitation of metal ions by sulphide ions, and in part explains the ability of these soils to act as sinks for heavy metals. Sulphides are produced under anaerobic conditions by sulphate-reducing bacteria, sulphate being the predominant form of sulphur in sea water. Although it shows considerable spatial variability, combined concentrations of S^{2-} and HS^- reached 0.1 mM at some points in the low salt marsh surface at Canvey Island in the Thames estuary (D. C. Havill, pers. comm.). The exact proportions of the reducing potential attributable to organic compounds in saltmarsh soils remain unknown. In waterlogged, paddy soils the organic products of anaerobic microbial metabolism can account for half of the total reducing potential. Organic compounds produced under these conditions include methane, ethane, ethene, fatty acids, aldehydes, ketones, alcohols, amines, mercaptans and heterocyclic compounds (Armstrong, 1976). Little information is currently available on the production of these compounds in saltmarsh soils, with the exception of methane which may be produced at rates of $9 \, \text{mg m}^{-2} \text{d}^{-1}$ during the summer (Drake and Read, 1981). Since their presence has been shown in both inland waterlogged soils and seabed sediments, it seems highly probable that all are also present in saltmarsh soils. Recently, Balba and Nedwell (1982) have shown substantial rates of fatty acid formation in the sediment below salt pans which in the surface 4 cm contained 5.3 mM acetate and 0.2 mM butyrate. Concentrations of CO_2 in the gas trapped within these soils also reach high levels, ranging from 2.5–4.2 % (Chapman, 1974a).

In conclusion it is difficult to envisage a habitat more hostile than that of a saltmarsh soil. Salinity is high and may fluctuate considerably in the upper marsh, presenting problems for osmoregulation. The soil is commonly anaerobic, accumulating a range of toxins and apparently acting as a sink for heavy metals. Nitrogen, and to a lesser extent phosphorus, are low by comparison to other soils. The only positive factors are a good supply of water, albeit saline, with frequent replenishment of K, Mg, Ca and many of the trace elements required by living organisms.

CHAPTER THREE

SALTMARSH FLORA

To survive on a salt marsh a species must withstand frequent inundations in sea water, soils which are often waterlogged, and mechanical damage by waves. Despite the harshness of the environment a number of species possess the combination of characters necessary for survival, although it will be clear from the preceding chapter that somewhat different selective pressures will operate in the different physiographical regions of a salt marsh. This chapter considers these plants, where they occur within the salt marsh, how they are adapted to their environment and how they may interact, both with individuals of their own species and other species, to produce putative successional changes.

3.1 Plant communities

Diversity

An examination of the floras of salt marshes throughout the world shows that most species will belong to a few cosmopolitan genera. For example, the genera *Salicornia*[1] (glassworts), *Spartina* (cord-grasses), *Juncus* (rushes), *Plantago* (plantains) and *Limonium* (sea-lavenders) are all widespread in both hemispheres and in the New and Old Worlds. Some of these genera are ecologically restricted to saline habitats, e.g. *Salicornia* and *Limonium*, whilst other genera include many species native to non-saline habitats, e.g. *Juncus* and *Plantago*.

If we take any one of these genera we will find a surprising geographical and ecological range. *Salicornia europaea* is common at the lowest levels of salt marshes in W. Europe, while *S. australis* and *S. virginica* occupy similar niches in New Zealand and California, respectively. Within the same

---

[1] Nomenclature for W. European vascular plants follows Clapham *et al.* (1962). Where this differs from Tutin *et al.* (1964–1980) the name given under this system is presented in parentheses at the first occurrence within the text. All other names are as cited in the source references.

marshes other *Salicornia* species may be found at higher levels. In W. Europe *S. perennis* (= *Anthrocnemum perenne*) may be found in the higher zones of the salt marsh, while *S. ambigua* and *S. subterminalis* are found in similar niches in New Zealand and California respectively (Chapman, 1977; Macdonald, 1977).

A number of species also show a remarkable range. The cord-grass *Spartina alterniflora* occurs along the east coast of North America from the tropics to the Bay of Fundy, where it survives for 4 months below 0°C each year. Yet throughout this climatic range it is commonly the dominant plant of the lower levels of the salt marsh (Long and Woolhouse, 1979). *Triglochin maritima* (sea-arrow grass) is common in the middle zones of salt marshes in W. Europe, but is also found in salt marshes of the Atlantic coast of Canada, Hudson Bay, the Pacific coast from Alaska to California and the coasts of Japan and China (Chapman, 1977; Macdonald, 1977; Jefferies *et al.*, 1979*b*).

Classification

Although saltmarsh composition, as in other vegetation types, shows an essentially continuous pattern of variation in space, it may be useful to delineate some groupings along this continuum in a classificatory system. Much early saltmarsh research in Europe concentrated on description and classification of vegetation. The classificatory system used in Britain was that of Tansley (1949) in which communities are subjectively assessed and a dominant species identified. Thus if *Puccinellia maritima* dominated an area of salt marsh, that species would characterize the area or community which would be called a *Puccinellietum*. Classification according to dominants has been used by Chapman (1976, 1977) in his classifications of saltmarsh communities throughout the world. This approach has been criticized by Adam (1978, 1981) because concentration on dominant species takes no account of the minor components, so that communities may be totally different in composition except for their dominant species. Elsewhere in Europe vegetation classification has followed the Braun–Blanquet or "Zurich–Montpellier" schools of plant sociology where groups are characterized according to their full species composition without emphasis on dominants. Using this system, Westhoff and Schouten (1979) provide a classification of the coastal communities of Europe, and Adam (1981) provides a detailed classification of British saltmarsh vegetation into 49 communities. Researchers in North America have been less pre-occupied with classificatory systems, although Macdonald (1977) has shown that the salt marshes of the Pacific coast may be floristically separated into five groups.

Zonation

A single salt marsh may include a number of communities. Although some may occur at the same altitude, a dominant factor in their arrangement will be the tidal or altitudinal zones. In many accounts of saltmarsh vegetation three basic zones may be recognized—low, middle and upper marsh (section 1.2). These boundaries are relative rather than absolute criteria. The "low marsh" is the lowest part of the marsh, the so-called pioneer zone, typically between MHWN and MHW. "Middle marsh" corresponds to the zone between MHW and MHWS, while the "high marsh" corresponds to the zone above MHWS. However, this varies with tidal amplitude and wave action. On a shore with a large tidal amplitude, exposed to wave action, the low marsh may begin close to MHW whilst on a sheltered shore with a narrow tidal amplitude the low marsh may start close to MLWN (Beeftink, 1977). A better guide is to divide the vertical range of the marsh, from the seaward limit to the highest point of influence of the tidal waters, into three equal vertical zones, i.e. low, middle and high (cf. Fig. 1.3). The species occupying these zones in a salt marsh of the Canadian Arctic, E. England and California are compared in Fig. 3.1. Despite the climatic and geographical contrasts all three salt marshes show a similar pattern of zonation. The low marsh includes only 3–4 species, one of which is far more abundant than the others, and there are significant bare areas. The middle marsh contains many more species and the major low marsh species are either absent or have a reduced cover. The higher marsh represents a mixture of halophytic and non-halophytic species. One notice-able difference between the sites is that on the Arctic site, in common with other Arctic marshes (Kershaw, 1976; Jefferies, 1977), species not generally considered as halophytes, such as *Carex aquatilis*, may be found on the middle marsh while the high marsh vegetation is almost 100% non-halo-phyte. In the California marsh the high level is predominantly halophytic. In the Arctic site high precipitation and low evapotranspiration result in a large freshwater input pushing the limit of seawater influence seaward, whilst in California, low precipitation and high evapotranspiration result in an extension of the influence of sea water inland.

Plant distribution, however, is not simply a reflection of altitude within the salt marsh. At a given height within the marsh a spatial variation also exists, which may often be related to physiographical features. In the

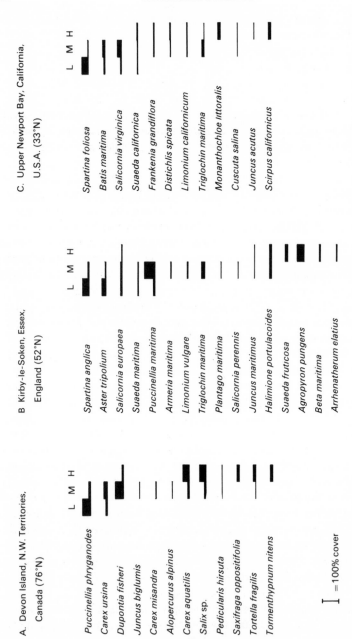

Figure 3.1 Ground area covered by different plant species in low (L), middle (M) and high (H) levels of three salt marshes in contrasting latitudinal locations. Data for (A) from Jefferies (1977), (B) from Long (unpublished) and (C) from Vogl (1966).

middle levels of salt marsh in E. England dense growths of *Halimione portulacoides* (sea purslane) may often be found fringing creeks, whilst it may be largely absent from less well drained areas at the same level, but distant from the creeks. In these poorly drained areas a low growth of a mixture of species may be found, including *Limonium vulgare* (sea lavender), *Armeria maritima* (thrift), *Plantago maritima* (sea plantain), *Triglochin maritima* (sea arrow grass) and short forms of *Puccinellia maritima* (sea meadow grass). Othman (1980), at Colne Point in E. England, examined the transition between two such areas, in which elevation varied less than 5 cm, by selecting 376 quadrats at random and classifying these according to species composition using the method of Williams and Lambert (1959). By this method quadrats are subdivided according to the presence or absence of the species showing the greatest degree of association with all other species. Six major groupings of quadrats were detected (Fig. 3.2*a*) and these could be related to distinct areas within the study site (Fig. 3.2*b*). Although these areas form a mosaic, a trend in their distribution is apparent with distance from the creek. The grouping, characterized by the presence of *Halimione portulacoides*, fringes the creek. Away from the creek a mixture of groupings characterized by either *H. portulacoides* or *P. maritima* or both is found. At about 20 m from the creek these are replaced by a grouping of quadrats which contain *Limonium vulgare*, *Armeria maritima*, *Triglochin maritima*, *Plantago maritima* and *Spergularia marina* with two groupings characterized by either the presence of *Spartina anglica* or of *Salicornia europaea* at the farthest point from the creek. Soils of the grouping characterized by *S. anglica* maintained the highest water contents for most of the year, had the lowest oxygen levels and showed both the highest and lowest salinities, depending on time of year. In contrast, the soils of the grouping characterized by *H. portulacoides* showed lower water contents, the highest oxygen levels and smaller fluctuations in salinity (Othman, 1980).

Such vegetational gradients within a given altitudinal zone may be found in most marshes. In the Atlantic coast marshes of the southern U.S.A., distinct differences in vegetation related to different physiographic features may be found. In the middle marsh, creeks are fringed with tall phenotypes of *Spartina alterniflora* reaching 2–3 m in height. The height of the *S. alterniflora* on the marsh flat diminishes with distance from the creek to short phenotypes of 60 cm or less, mixed with *Salicornia* and *Limonium* spp. This vegetation is replaced by *Distichlis spicata*, with *Salicornia* spp. on sandy areas or by *Juncus roemerianus* where a regular seepage of fresh water into the marsh occurs (Cooper, 1974).

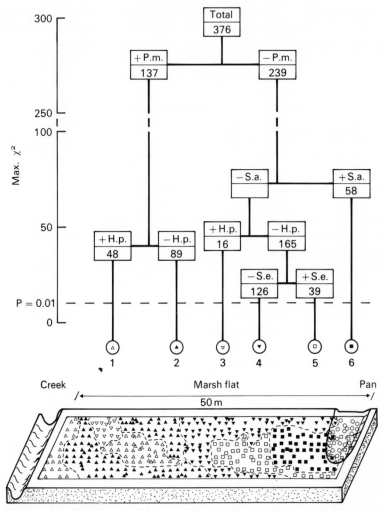

Figure 3.2 (a) Hierarchical classification of 376 quadrats of 10 cm × 10 cm selected by a randomized block design from an area of 10 m by 50 m on the middle marsh at Colne Point, E. England. Species upon which the classification is based are plotted against the sum of the chi-square values obtained by comparison with all other species in the quadrat group. The characteristic species are *Puccinellia maritima* (P.m.), *Spartina anglica* (S.a.), *Halimione portulacoides* (H.p.) and *Salicornia europaea* (S.e.). Grouping 4, 126 quadrats, was characterized by the absence of all four species, but represented a forb-rich community, including *Armeria maritima*, *Limonium vulgare*, *Triglochin maritima* and *Aster tripolium*. (b) Map illustrating the positions of each quadrat in the sample area and identifying its classificatory grouping. Open symbols indicate quadrats devoid of vascular plants; these were not included in the classification (after Othman, 1980).

In the lower zone of the salt marshes of East Pen Island, Hudson Bay, a different vegetational gradient is found. The lower levels are dominated by *Puccinellia phryganodes* and *Carex subspathacea*, but the pans at this level, which would normally be devoid of vascular plants in warmer climates, are dominated by *Hippuris vulgaris, Senecio congestus* and *Ranunculus hyperboreus* (Kershaw, 1976).

Non-vascular plants

Vegetation descriptions of salt marshes have concentrated on vascular plants, not only because they are the more obvious component of the vegetation, but also because their presence defines the seaward limit of the salt marsh (p. 1). However, a few species of Bryophyta and many algae also form significant components of the vegetation. Adam (1976) lists 72 species of Bryophyta found on salt marshes in Britain, but only one species, *Pottia heimii*, was more frequent in saltmarsh sites than elsewhere. In general, Bryophyta are limited to the higher levels of the marsh, and in Britain are more predominant on the west coast marshes where higher precipitation would result in less saline conditions. In a salt marsh on Devon Island, Arctic Canada, Jefferies (1977) reported five species of Bryophyta in the upper marsh, constituting nearly half of the total cover.

In contrast to the Bryophyta, macroscopic algae tend to predominate at the lower levels of the salt marsh. Although generally regarded as characteristic of rocky shores, forms of some of the large algae are also able to colonize saltmarsh habitats. In Britain, free-floating forms of the green seaweed *Enteromorpha intestinalis* are frequently washed into salt pans, where they can grow rapidly whilst a pool persists or until washed out by a high tide. *Pelvetia canaliculata* ecad *libera* is also found in pans and entangled among vascular plant stems in the upper levels of the marsh. Other species such as *Enteromorpha nana* and *Catanella repens* are epiphytic, clinging to the stems of vascular plants. Dwarf forms of bladderwrack, *Fucus vesiculosus*, and knotted wrack, *Ascophyllum nodosum*, are commonly found interspersed with vascular plants in the lower salt marsh, often anchored in mud accreted around the vascular plant stems. In comparison to their counterparts on rocky shores these forms are stunted and usually lack airbladders. In general, the forms of macro-algae found on salt marshes are morphologically distinct from forms of the same species found on rocky shores. These differences appear to result from phenotypic plasticity rather than a genotypic difference; thus these forms are termed ecads, rather than ecotypes, subspecies, or varieties. Brinkhuis and Jones (1976) demonstrated that the dwarf *Ascophyllum nodosum* ecad *scorpoides*, collected from among the stems of *Spartina alterniflora* on an Atlantic coast marsh of the U.S.A., grew into the larger, bladdered form typical of open habitats when transplanted to lower levels of the shore. Similarly, *Pelvetia canaliculata*, removed from a rocky shore in Anglesey, Wales, and transplanted to a nearby salt marsh assumed the growth form of the saltmarsh phenotype within three months (De Oliveira and Fletcher, 1980).

A wide range of small algae may be found in all but the driest parts of the salt marsh. Despite the twice-daily scouring by the tides, filamentous golden-brown algae (Chrysophyta), such as *Vaucheria thuretii*, are able to colonize steep creek banks, probably anchoring themselves by means of rhizoids (Chapman, 1976). Rich *Vaucheria* communities have been reported in the Solway marshes, Scotland, and the Wadden area (Polderman and Polderman-Hall, 1980). Blue-green algae (Cyanophyta) such as the filamentous *Calothrix* spp. and the jelly-like blobs of *Rivularia* spp., may be found in the shelter of vascular plants. On exposed mud between vascular plants on the lower shore a community dominated by the unbranched filamentous green alga, *Ulothrix*, is commonly found in the spring, but disappears in the summer, and at higher levels in the marsh is replaced by a mixed community of Cyanophyta including *Oscillatoria*, *Phormidium*, *Lyngbya*, and *Microcoleus*, often with an accompanying diatom flora. Such a community has been described from marshes in Europe, N. America and New Zealand (Chapman, 1977). In common with the vascular plants, zonation of the algal species in relation to frequency of tidal inundation has been observed on several salt marshes (Chapman, 1974).

3.2 Adaptation to environmental stress

The dominant factor determining the composition of saltmarsh flora is the ability to withstand seawater inundation. The most obvious, and indeed the defining, characteristic of saltmarsh vegetation is its ability to withstand high soil salinities. Salinity tolerance is not only a prerequisite for survival in a salt marsh, but the degree of tolerance is an important factor determining the distributional limits of a species within the salt marsh.

Salinity

Soil salinity in salt marshes and its relation to sea water have been described earlier (Fig. 2.11). Effects of salinity on the physiology of plants may be classified as osmotic, nutritional and directly toxic (Bernstein, 1964).

Both the osmotic potential (ψ_π) and the water potential (ψ) of oceanic water are approximately $-2.0\,\text{MPa}$ (1 MPa or megapascal = 10 bars = c. 10 atmospheres pressure). To survive inundation in this water a plant must maintain an internal water potential (ψ_i) of $-2.0\,\text{MPa}$ or below. In most crop plants protein and DNA synthesis are inhibited when $\psi_i < -0.5\,\text{MPa}$, and the wilting point will commonly be reached at $\psi_i = -1.5\,\text{MPa}$ (Hsaio, 1973), yet saltmarsh plants must maintain an even lower ψ_i, below $-2.0\,\text{MPa}$, simply to prevent their dehydration.

Salinity also affects plant mineral nutrition. Chloride is an essential micronutrient for all plants. Sodium is required by those plants which utilize the C_4 pathway of photosynthetic carbon metabolism; this grouping includes the saltmarsh genera *Spartina* and *Distichlis* (Brownell, 1979; Long et al., 1975; Winter, 1979). Neither Na^+ or Cl^- on the other hand is required at more than about 500 mM, but sea water contains about a thousand times this concentration. Some plants, e.g. sugar beet, which can grow without sodium, nevertheless show growth stimulation in the presence of low concentrations of sodium and growth retardation in the presence of high concentrations (Jennings, 1968). This pattern of response may also be seen in saltmarsh plants, e.g. *Aster tripolium* var. *discoideus* and *Spartina anglica* (Fig. 3.3). *A. tripolium* shows maximal growth at salinities of about 20 mM, above which growth is progressively inhibited. At 200 mM relative growth rate is less than half of that in non-saline media. Yet these rates are for material collected from the lowest levels of a salt marsh, showing that the presence of the species is clearly a result of tolerance rather than a requirement for high salinities. Growth analysis reveals that growth at low salinities is decreased by a reduction in the amount of leaf area formed. Only at high salinities is the assimilatory capacity per unit of leaf area reduced.

Elevated Na^+ and Cl^- levels may influence the uptake of other ions. High concentrations of Na^+ have been shown to depress K^+ uptake both in halophytes such as *Jaumea carnosa* (St. Omer and Schlesinger, 1980) and non-halophytes such as *Hordeum vulgare* (Storey and Wyn Jones, 1978). Elevated levels of NaCl may induce K^+ and other nutrient deficiencies in plants growing on soils that would otherwise be considered to have adequate levels of available mineral nutrients (Solav'ev, 1969).

A final effect of salinity is direct toxicity to metabolism by the elevated levels of ions. In cell-free extracts of both the saltmarsh species *Suaeda maritima* and the salt-sensitive species *Pisum sativum* (pea), protein

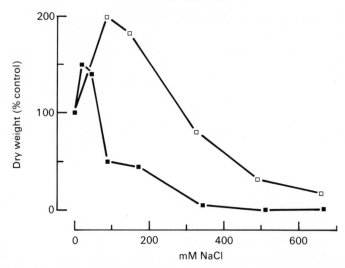

Figure 3.3   Dry weight, as a percentage of control, of seedlings of *Aster tripolium* (closed symbols) and *Spartina anglica* (open symbols) after *c.* 40 days' growth in a range of salinities of the rooting medium.

synthesis, oxidative phosphorylation, and a number of enzymes are strongly and similarly inhibited by 200 mM of NaCl. Studies of a range of saltmarsh species have shown that *Suaeda maritima* is no exception (Flowers *et al.*, 1977). Osmond and Greenway (1972) obtained similar results in a comparison of enzymes of salt-tolerant *Atriplex hastata* and salt-sensitive *Phaseolus vulgaris*. The only exception to this pattern is the observation that photosynthetic electron transport in isolated chloroplast thylakoids of the mangrove *Rhizophora mucronata* is strongly stimulated by added NaCl, with an optimum at 500 mM (Critchley, 1982).

In summary, for a species to survive regular inundation in sea water it must maintain a low water potential, presumably by concentration of solutes, but at the same time exclude Na^+ and Cl^- from sites of active metabolism.

Mechanisms of salinity tolerance

How do saltmarsh plants maintain a water potential sufficiently below that of the saltmarsh soil to allow water uptake from the saline soil water? The water potential of mature plant cells is determined by two major components:

$$\psi_i = \psi_p + \psi_\pi \tag{3.1}$$

where ψ_i = the internal or cell water potential
        ψ_p = the hydrostatic pressure or turgor pressure potential
        ψ_π = the osmotic potential

ψ_p is the pressure exerted on the protoplast by the rigid plant cell wall, which varies from zero in the flaccid cells of wilted plants to 1.0–2.0 MPa in fully turgid cells. ψ_π is zero for pure water and decreases with increased solute concentration. Since the water of cells is never pure, ψ_π will always be negative. In practice, cell and plant water potential range from just below zero, $c. -0.1$ MPa to -1.5 MPa, in mesophytes, and as low as -6.1 MPa in some desert and saltmarsh plants.

The water potential of sea water is approximately -2.0 MPa. The flux of water (J_v) into root cells will be proportional to the difference between the water potentials outside and inside $(J_v \propto \psi_0 - \psi_i)$. Thus ψ_i must be below -2.0 MPa if a plant whose roots are flooded with sea water is to survive. Since a significant ψ_p of 0.5–1.0 MPa must be maintained for root growth and other processes, ψ_π must, by reference to eqn. 3.1, be less than -3.0 MPa to obtain the required ψ_i (Dainty, 1979). Within the plant the same reasoning applies, i.e. to move water from the root to the shoot, the shoot must maintain a ψ_i below that of the root. In non-halophytes, normal protoplasmic concentrations of K^+ of about 100–200 mM are found and thought to be necessary for cellular activity (Dainty, 1979). To achieve the required ψ_i within a saltmarsh plant, a salt concentration of about 600 mM KCl, or osmotically equivalent concentration of other solutes, would be needed (Dainty, 1979). Analyses of the ionic contents of saltmarsh plants suggest that the bulk of this 600 mM salt concentration is NaCl. Many saltmarsh species accumulate high concentrations of NaCl in their shoots and roots (Table 3.1). In *Salicornia rubra* Na^+ and Cl^- accounted for between 75% and 93% of ψ_π, whilst K^+, Ca^{2+}, PO_4^{3-} and NO_3^- together accounted for less than 1% (Flowers *et al.*, 1977). However, as noted earlier, many cellular processes of saltmarsh plants are strongly inhibited by NaCl and all available evidence suggests that 600 mM NaCl in the cytoplasm would be catastrophic. In mature cells, the vacuole

Table 3.1 Na^+ contents (μmoles g dwt^{-1}) of shoots and roots of seedlings grown for 37 days in 400 mM NaCl (after Yaakub, 1980).

	Shoot	Root
Aster tripolium	410 ± 20	200 ± 10
Spartina anglica	140 ± 5	120 ± 6

occupies 90–95% of the cell volume and 600 mM NaCl here would not present a problem since it is not a site of active metabolism. Ion efflux analyses of *Suaeda maritima* grown in water culture with 340 mM NaCl suggested vacuolar concentrations in leaf cells of 600 mM Na^+ and cytoplasmic concentrations of 165 mM. In general, inorganic ion concentrations in the cytoplasm of cells of saltmarsh plants appear similar to those in non-halophytes. The chloroplast may however be an exception. It has been suggested that chloroplasts of *Limonium vulgare* accumulate Na^+ and Cl^- to 500 and 700 mM (Flowers *et al.*, 1977). This is of particular interest in view of Critchley's (1982) recent observation that maximal photosynthetic electron transport in one halophyte is achieved at 500 mM Cl^-.

If there is an imbalance in ion concentrations between the cytoplasm and vacuole the cytoplasm must maintain a ψ equal to that of the vacuole if it is not to be dehydrated by the vacuole. Many saltmarsh plants accumulate proline or betaines in response to increased rooting medium salinity (Storey *et al.*, 1979; Stewart *et al.*, 1979). Some taxa appear to accumulate only proline, others only betaines, and others both or neither (Table 3.2). *Plantago maritima* accumulates the polyhydric alcohol sorbitol in response to increased rooting medium salinity (Stewart *et al.*, 1979). However, accumulation of these compounds varies with time of year and with salinity (Jefferies *et al.*, 1979a). *Limonium vulgare* grown in 200 mM

Table 3.2 Proline and methylated quaternary ammonium compounds (MQAC) in plants collected from salt marshes in N. Wales and N.W. England (μmoles g fwt^{-1}) (after Stewart *et al.*, 1979). Methylated quaternary ammonium compounds are (1) glycine betaine, (2) homobetaine and (3) dimethyl propiothetin with glycine betaine.

	Proline	MQAC
Agropyron pungens	< 5	80(1)
Halimione portulacoides	< 5	50(1)
Salicornia europaea	< 5	50(1)
Glaux maritima	31	< 5(1)
Puccinellia maritima	60	< 5(1)
Triglochin maritima	72	< 5(1)
Agrostis stolonifera	40	15(1)
Armeria maritima	38	32(2)
Limonium vulgare	60	40(2)
Spartina anglica	16	80(3)
Juncus maritimus	< 5	< 5(1)
Plantago maritima	< 5	< 5(1)

NaCl accumulates more homobetaine than proline whilst at 600 mM NaCl more proline is accumulated (Stewart *et al.*, 1979). *In vitro*, high concentrations of these solutes of up to 2000 mM have no effect on the function of enzymes tested. The observed concentrations of these solutes appear sufficient, if they are confined to the cytoplasm, to provide the required osmotic balance between the cytoplasm and vacuole (Dainty, 1979). However, even though this will provide osmotic equilibrium, large ion gradients will exist between the vacuole and the cytoplasm. Energy will be needed both to accumulate NaCl in the vacuole against an electro-chemical gradient and to maintain the gradient. The vacuolar membranes in non-halophytes are considered to be relatively leaky, i.e. allow passive diffusion of ions. If this is true of halophytes then there could be a consider-able expenditure of energy involved in simply pumping ions back out of the cytoplasm.

One final problem that the saltmarsh environment presents to plant water relations is continual change in the soil salinity. On the higher marsh, soil salinities may rise in dry periods to concentrations above those of sea water, while after heavy rainfall the salinities may drop considerably below that of sea water. In these circumstances a plant with a high inter-nal solute concentration will take up water, swelling its protoplasts, the expansion of which will be checked by the hydrostatic pressure exerted by the wall. Consider a plant which has adapted to the external water potential of sea water and assume that it has an internal osmotic potential of $\psi_\pi = -3.0$ MPa. If heavy rainfall now occurs and rapidly decreases the external ψ to zero, equilibrium may only be obtained when $\psi_p = 3.0$ MPa (eqn. 3.1), i.e., a pressure 30 times that of the atmosphere would be applied to the cell walls. One method by which this stress could be ameliorated would be if the cell walls were sufficiently elastic to allow the uptake of water. If the average cell volume, for example, could double then the hydrostatic pressure required at equilibrium would be halved. Clearly, the ability to tolerate such pressure changes at the cellular level will be an important attribute of saltmarsh plants. In the longer term, plants may adapt to reduced external salinities by a decrease in their solute con-centrations.

The general pattern of adaptation to low soil water potentials in many saltmarsh plants appears to be an accumulation of salts, principally Na^+ and Cl^- in the shoot, together with the synthesis of smaller concentrations of organic solutes. This contrasts with many non-halophytes where tolerance appears to depend on exclusion of salts from the shoot. Here, decreased soil water potential would need to be counteracted by increased concentration of organic solutes in the shoot (Greenway and Munns, 1980). Nevertheless, at least one saltmarsh plant shows this strategy. Rozema and Blom (1977) found that in *Juncus gerardii* and *Agrostis stolonifera*, collected from the same site in the upper marsh and then grown in flooded substrate with 50 % sea water, the shoot Na concentration in the former was three times that of the root but was little more than half the root concentration in the latter. Different ecotypes of *Agrostis stolonifera* may be found at a variety of inland sites and in the high levels of salt marsh. At all salinities, uptake of NaCl into the shoot was lower in the saltmarsh than inland ecotypes, while the saltmarsh ecotype showed greater accumulation of organic solutes, especially glycine betaine, in response to increased salinity (Ahmad *et al.*, 1981). In summary, there may be two strategies of adaptation. Firstly, to exclude NaCl at the root level and compensate for the low external ψ by the generation of organic solutes in the shoot as exemplified by *Agrostis stolonifera*. Alternatively, NaCl may be accumulated in the shoot, providing the bulk of the osmotic balance, but efficiently compartmented in the vacuoles of the shoot cells and organic solutes, providing the osmotic balance in the cytoplasm, e.g. in *Suaeda maritima*.

However, all saltmarsh plants must regulate their salt content to prevent the accumulation of unnecessarily high and energetically expensive concentrations in the vacuole and to increase tissue osmotic potential in response to rising soil water potentials. That regulation must occur will be apparent if we consider the transpiration stream.

For every kg of dry matter produced, between $0.280 \, m^3$ and $0.840 \, m^3$ of water is lost in transpiration, for a range of herbaceous plants (Larcher, 1975). If there were no barriers to salt uptake and no mechanisms for removing the salt we can extrapolate to deduce that in saltmarsh plants growing on soils with dissolved salt concentrations of $7–50 \, kg \, m^{-3}$, the inorganic salt contents would range from 66 % to 98 %! The fact that salt contents do not approach these levels is evidence of the existence of mechanisms of exclusion and/or removal. Mechanisms of regulating salt concentration in saltmarsh plants may be classified, as exclusion, shedding and dilution.

Uptake of NaCl in the transpiration stream is limited by a barrier in the root system. The main barrier to passive uptake of NaCl into the shoots is almost certainly the suberized endodermis of the root. At this location nearly all the water has to flow through cell membranes with a very low permeability to Na^+ and Cl^- (Greenway and Munns, 1980). These membranes may have outwardly directed Na^+ pumps which could further limit salt concentration in the root (Dainty, 1979). However, it is clear that this barrier is not 100% efficient and, for the many saltmarsh plants which accumulate NaCl in their shoots, it is obviously important that it should not be so.

Salt within the shoot may be shed in two ways: active excretion, and loss through the death of tissues. A number of genera of saltmarsh vascular plants have been shown to possess glands or bladders, which are associated with the epidermis of the leaves or stem and actively secrete salt; these include Spartina, Armeria, Limonium, and Glaux (Lüttge, 1975; Rozema et al., 1981). Hill (1967a, b) has studied the physiology of the salt-gland of Limonium vulgare collected from salt marshes in E. England. Each gland may excrete up to $0.5 \, mm^3$ of salt solution in an hour. Analyses of the electrical and concentration gradients across the glands show that the ions are driven against an electrochemical gradient, i.e. energy must be expended by the plant to excrete the salt. Analysis of the conduction of current across the gland by Cl^- in association with a membrane-impermeable cation and by Na^+ in association with a membrane-impermeable anion, suggested that salt excretion was achieved via an electrogenic Cl^- pump with an affinity for Na^+ and K^+. In other words Cl^- is actively pumped out of the gland cells on to the leaf surface, presumably at the expense of ATP. The electrical gradient produced across the membrane will then passively drag the cations Na^+ and K^+ across the membrane. Salt-glands in Limonium are separated from the other leaf cells by the cuticle, the only contact being protoplasmic connections (Fig. 3.4a). Thus in Limonium salt can only leave the leaf by crossing the cytoplasm. Structurally, the salt-glands of Spartina are quite different (Fig. 3.4b) and their cell walls are in hydraulic contact with those of the mesophyll. Histological studies of ion movement through these salt-glands have shown that, in contrast to Limonium, movement is primarily through the cell walls (Lüttge, 1975). When exposed to 100 mM concentrations of different salts, Spartina anglica showed an excretion rate in the presence of NaCl three and twelve times greater than in the presence of KCl and $CaCl_2$, respectively, the reduction in cation and chloride excretion rates being similar. Limonium vulgare showed only a slight reduction in excretion rate with KCl by comparison with NaCl (Rozema et al., 1981). The results indicate that Na^+ is more likely to be the ion actively extruded in the salt-gland of Spartina. Analysis of salts excreted by leaves of Spartina alterniflora in the field suggest that Na^+ constitutes between 34–42%, K^+ 2%, and Ca^{2+} 0.1% of total salt dry weight. Interestingly some excretion of nutrients also occurs, since phosphate constituted about 0.01% of the solute (McGovern

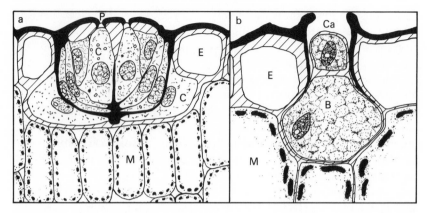

Figure 3.4 Transverse sections through the salt-glands of leaves. (a) *Limonium vulgare* (× 500) consisting of 24 cells in total (8 illustrated) with collecting cells (C) in contact with the mesophyll (M) below and with the gland cells above via numerous plasmodesmata crossing the cuticular extensions, which are indicated by black ink. Salt solution is excreted on to the leaf surface through pores (P) in the cuticle (after Lüttge, 1975). (b) *Spartina anglica* (× 2000) consisting of two cells in total with a single basal cell (B) in contact with the mesophyll (M) and with the smaller cap cell (Ca) which excretes salt solution through a single pore on to the leaf surface.

et al., 1979). Species clearly differ in the effectiveness of their salt-glands. The efficiency of salt secretion may be defined by the ratio of the rates of ion secretion and the rate of change in internal ion concentration. For plants grown in 150 mM NaCl the relative efficiencies of Na excretion were 1.0–1.5 for *Spartina anglica*, 0.3–0.5 for *Limonium vulgare* and 0.04 for *Armeria maritima* (Rozema *et al.*, 1981). The high efficiency reported here for *Spartina* may, in part, explain why species of this genus are, throughout the temperate zones, so commonly found in the lowest levels of salt marshes, i.e. the sites most frequently inundated by sea water.

No evidence of salt-glands has been found in other prominent saltmarsh genera, notably *Puccinellia*, *Juncus*, *Suaeda* and *Salicornia*. In species both with and without salt-glands a significant method of salt regulation may be through the shedding of dead, salt-saturated leaves and stems (Albert, 1975). Plants of *Spartina anglica* and *Aster tripolium* grown in 130 mM NaCl over a 17-day period lost, via the shedding of dead leaves, 42 % and 3 % respectively of the Na^+ taken up by the plants (Yaakub, 1980). Succulence, shown most notably by species of *Salicornia*, but also by many other dicotyledonous species of salt marshes, is a further method of regulation of internal salt concentration. These species respond to the presence of NaCl by developing cells of greater volume in the shoots. In effect, high concentrations of ions in the shoot are prevented by dilution in the increased water content of the cells (Jennings, 1968).

One final factor that may effectively decrease salt uptake is transpiration. The greater the transpirational loss of water from a plant the greater the flux of saline water into its root system. The majority of saltmarsh plants show morphological features that would limit transpiration, i.e. they are xeromorphic. Leaves of *Spartina anglica* and *S. alterniflora* bear a thick cuticle and their stomata are limited to the base of deep grooves in the upper surface. The leaves of *Puccinellia maritima* are capable of rolling to enclose the stoma-bearing surface. *Salicornia* spp. have essentially adopted the morphological strategy of the cacti. Their leaves are totally reduced and the main photosynthetic organs, the stems, are round and sausage-shaped, so minimizing the surface to volume ratio. Plants utilizing the C_4 pathway of photosynthesis show increased water-use efficiencies when compared to morphologically similar species using the C_3 pathway of photosynthesis. Typically a C_4 plant will transpire roughly half of the water transpired by an equivalent C_3 plant for each unit mass of dry weight formed (Downes, 1969). At inland sites, C_4 species are very rare outside of the tropics and sub-tropics, but on salt marshes C_4 species are found in temperate regions where they include some of the most abundant species, notably all species of the grass genera *Spartina* and *Distichlis*, and some species of the Chenopodiaceae, e.g. *Suaeda fruticosa* (= *S. vera*) and *Atriplex laciniata* (Winter, 1979; Long and Woolhouse, 1979). C_4 photosynthesis may serve as a mechanism for decreasing transpiration and thus limiting salt intake.

Waterlogging

A second effect of tidal inundation for significant areas of salt marsh is waterlogging. Waterlogging is characteristic of the lower marsh, inundated by the majority of tides. Where the drainage of flooding water is impeded, waterlogging will be common in the middle and even high marsh.

The effects of waterlogging on saltmarsh soils were considered in the preceding chapter (p. 36). The basic effect of waterlogging is the production of anaerobic conditions in which a range of reduced inorganic and organic ions is produced. The combined anaerobic and reducing conditions produced by waterlogging are fatal to most plants of dry lands, including the majority of crops. Mild waterlogging may cause partial death of the root system and stunt root growth. The bases of these effects are multiple. Oxygen starvation in itself will kill roots. CO_2 concentrations above 1 % inhibit growth of many plants, and 9–10 % CO_2 for any period is fatal to roots (Russell, 1961). Concentrations within this range were found in the soils of the salt marshes at Scolt Head, E. England (Chapman, 1974a). A range of organic products is produced by anaerobic microbial metabolism (section 2.4) and of these the monocarboxylic acids are known to be directly phytotoxic, whilst ethylene, a plant growth inhibitor, prevents root elongation at concentrations of just $1 \mu g \, cm^{-3}$ (Armstrong, 1976). Many of the organic compounds produced are metabolic inhibitors and thus further phytotoxicity could be expected. Elements such as manganese and boron, which are toxic in high concentrations, are more readily available to plants in their reduced ionic states. The phytotoxic heavy metals copper, lead, mercury and zinc, which are unusually abundant in saltmarsh soils (p. 33), would also be more readily available under reducing conditions. This is demonstrated by the high concentrations of heavy metals found in some saltmarsh plants. For example, dried shoots of *Spartina alterniflora* collected from salt marshes near Beaufort in North Carolina contained zinc, manganese and iron levels averaging 22, 200 and $5000 \, mg \, kg^{-1}$, respectively (Williams and Murdoch, 1967). Some plants have a specific requirement of nitrate over other inorganic forms of nitrogen and thus loss of nitrate under reducing conditions may impair nitrogen metabolism. Finally, sulphide which is toxic to plant roots at concentrations as low as $1 \mu M$ will be locally abundant due to microbial transformation of organic matter by sulphite-reducing bacteria (Chapter 6). Which one, if any, of this multitude of phytotoxic effects of waterlogging is of importance in determining the distribution of plants within any part of the salt marsh will clearly be very difficult to unravel.

Die-back and growth reduction in *Spartina anglica* and *S. alterniflora* have been correlated with increased anaerobiosis (Goodman *et al.*, 1959; Howes *et al.*, 1981). Water culture experiments have suggested that the anaerobiosis itself could account for the stunting of *S. alterniflora* (Linthurst, 1980). Much emphasis has been placed on the redox potential of saltmarsh soils as a whole. However, it does not quantitatively show which redox pairs underlie this value or their relative concentrations. Brereton (1971) showed a correlation between the distribution of *Salicornia europaea* and redox on salt marshes at Foryd Bay, N. Wales. Havill (pers. comm.), at Canvey Island, E. England, found a significantly stronger relationship between *S. europaea* distribution and sulphide concentration than with redox. This suggests that a direct effect was more likely to be produced by sulphide, the weaker apparent relationship with redox being an indirect effect of a correlation between sulphide and redox.

A combination of two strategies is probably employed by saltmarsh plants in tolerating waterlogging; avoidance of anaerobiosis and bio-chemical tolerance. Saltmarsh plants avoid anaerobiosis either by rooting in the more aerated surface layers or by aerating the rhizosphere, i.e. the soil/root interface. *Spartina anglica* and *S. alterniflora* appear to combine both strategies. They produce a surface mat of fine roots which have poor internal aeration, and a system of "anchor" roots penetrating several centi-metres or even metres, which have a good internal aeration. Examination of a highly anaerobic, black saltmarsh soil, containing roots of *S. anglica*, will show an oxidized zone of 2–3 mm surrounding the root. This is characterized by an orange/red appearance due to the formation and precipitation of the more oxidized ferric form of iron in the locally aerobic rhizosphere. By creating an oxygenated zone around the root the com-bined toxic effects of waterlogging are avoided. Cylindrical platinum elec-trodes applied to these roots have shown that oxygen may diffuse rapidly through them (Armstrong, 1967; Baker, 1979). This may be explained by the very large and continuous air-filled cavities in the large roots of *S. anglica* and *S. alterniflora*. Extrapolating from the photographs of Anderson (1974), in a 2 mm diameter root of *S. alterniflora* 71% of the cross-sectional area was occupied by cavities in the aerenchyma of the root cortex. These cavities are typically large, with a mean diameter of about 0.5 mm in a 2 mm diameter root. Such cavities would have a very low resistance to gas diffusion and would thus allow the root to maintain a high oxygen content at several metres from the shoot.

Correspondingly large air spaces have been shown in the leaf sheaths of *S. alterniflora*, suggesting an efficient gas transport system from the shoots in the atmosphere to the roots at some distance below the marsh surface. Similarly, roots of *Distichlis spicata* and *Juncus roemerianus* show large air spaces in their roots, occupying 70% or more of the cross-sectional area, whilst roots of *Limonium* sp. and *Salicornia virginica* show smaller air spaces, occupying 15–20% of the root cross-sectional area (calculated from Anderson, 1974).

Mechanisms of biochemical adaptation to anaerobiosis in saltmarsh plants are poorly understood. It is, however, clear that they exist, since seeds of the saltmarsh species *Suaeda australis*, *Triglochin striata* and *Juncus maritimus* were all capable of germinating under 4 mm of water, whilst some germination occurred even under 5 cm of water (Ranwell, 1972). Saltmarsh populations of *Festuca rubra*, *Armeria maritima* and *Plantago maritima* are significantly more tolerant of Mn than inland populations (C. E. Singer, pers. comm.). Rice, which is normally grown in waterlogged soils, is able enzymically to oxidize toxins produced in the anaerobic soil (Armstrong, 1976). Recent research on *S. alterniflora* has shown that not only are the roots of this species well aerated, but they are also separately capable of metabolically raising the redox of their rhizo-sphere through enzymic oxidations (Howes *et al.*, 1981).

Submergence

A third effect of tidal inundation is physical submergence of the vegetation in flowing and often turbid waters. Effects of submergence may be classified as restriction of gaseous exchange between the plant and atmos-phere, shading, and mechanical damage.

Unlike the laminae of the macro-algae the shoots of the higher plants of the salt marsh are covered by a thick cuticle which will inhibit gaseous exchange between the shoot and submerging waters. The effectiveness of stomata will be greatly reduced during submergence by the very much lower diffusion coefficients of CO_2 and O_2 in water by comparison to air. This isolation of the plant from the atmosphere would largely prevent photosynthetic uptake of CO_2 in the light and may starve the plant of O_2. Aeration of the root system depends on oxygen diffusion into the soil surface and into the air spaces of the deeper roots via the shoot. During submergence both sources of oxygen will be restricted. Thus, to survive submergence, the root system must have a sufficient reservoir of oxygen to endure the period of submergence or the capacity to withstand temporary anaerobiosis of the tissues. However, if sufficient light is able to penetrate the submerging waters, then photosynthesis, utilizing CO_2 generated by shoot and root respiration, would recycle the O_2 and may prevent tissue anaerobiosis. One mechanism of decreasing the restriction on gaseous exchange resulting from submergence is the trapping of an air film over the leaf during submergence. This will increase the effective surface area for gaseous exchange between the submerging waters and the leaf, and allow the stomata to function effectively. Because of its cuticular sculpturing and surface invagination the upper surface of leaves of *Spartina anglica* and other species of the genus traps such an air layer on submergence. The stomata in these leaves are confined to the upper surface (Long, 1976). This might, in part, explain why in the clear tidal waters of Poole Harbour, S. England, this species has become established down to MLWN, where the plants may be submerged for 16 h day^{-1} (Hubbard, 1969).

However, if the submerging waters are turbid, light penetration will be impeded and thus photosynthesis prevented. At the relatively sheltered sites in Hamford Water and the Stour Estuary, E. England, *S. anglica* is restricted to sites above MHWN and here light penetration is restricted by the turbid waters, which can absorb 80 % of the incident visible light in the surface 5 cm (Dunn, 1981; Long, unpublished). The most turbid tidal waters in Britain are perhaps those of the Fal estuary, W. England, which carry sediment resulting from china clay extraction (Ranwell, 1972). Even on the most sheltered parts of this estuary saltmarsh plants are limited to the zone above MHW.

Despite the sheltered positions which are a prerequisite of saltmarsh formation, marsh surfaces and their plants will be subjected occasionally to wave action during storms, besides the currents of the ebbing and flowing tides. The most extreme form of mechanical damage will be complete removal of the plant from the marsh surface. Clearly, seedlings will be most vulnerable. Chapman (1974a) suggests that *Aster tripolium* requires five days of continuous exposure following germination for the seedlings to reach sufficient size to resist removal by the tides. This would limit the seaward extent of *A. tripolium* to just above MHWN. Mature plants may resist uprooting by the development of a deep root system such as the anchor roots of *Spartina* spp. (Anderson, 1974), the extensive woody rhizomes of *Halimione portulacoides* or woody rootstock of *Limonium* spp. Succulence, induced by salinity, will also decrease the probability of uprooting since the decreased surface to volume ratio will effectively streamline the plant, so decreasing frictional drag and the transfer of momentum from the moving water to the plant.

Anatomically and morphologically many saltmarsh plants may be seen to be adapted to resist mechanical damage by water action. Most leaves possess thick cuticles, collenchyma and often sclerenchyma (Anderson, 1974), which will greatly increase the mechanical strength of the leaves. Leaves are often small or narrow, so minimizing resistance to flowing water. A number of genera, e.g. *Limonium, Armeria* and *Plantago*, are low-growing. This would also minimize mechanical damage, since frictional drag in moving water will be greatest at the surface, and the current together with the danger of mechanical damage will increase with height above the marsh surface.

3.3   Intraspecific variation and interactions

It will be clear from the preceding discussion that there is considerable interspecific variation in the methods and degrees of tolerance to the saltmarsh environment. Large-scale environmental gradients occur across the marsh and more subtle gradients occur within the different levels of marsh. A single species is rarely restricted to one part of the marsh. *Aster tripolium* may commonly be found on the low, middle and high levels of salt marshes in Britain (Gray *et al.*, 1979). Similarly, *Spartina anglica*, although most frequent in the low levels, may also be found in the poorly drained soils fringing salt pans in the middle levels of W. European salt marshes (Othman, 1980; Meesenburg, 1971). *Spartina alterniflora* shows a similar pattern in New England salt marshes (Shea *et al.*, 1975). Many other species may be shown to span two or even all three levels in the salt marsh (Jefferies *et al.*, 1981; Gray *et al.*, 1979). Indeed, a few species can occur not only at different levels in the salt marsh but also at non-saline inland sites. For example, *Armeria maritima* in W. Europe occurs both on the middle and upper levels of salt marshes and on mountains inland.

Within a single marsh individuals of a species may show marked morphological and phenological differences. The tall and short forms of *Spartina alterniflora* respectively associated with creeks and marsh flat in the east coast marshes of the U.S.A. are perhaps the best known example. Populations of *Salicornia europaea*, *Triglochin maritima* and *Aster tripolium* on low and high marsh at Stiffkey, E. England, showed very different seasonal patterns of growth (Jefferies and Perkins, 1977). The low marsh populations showed continuous growth through the summer, whilst the high marsh populations showed little growth during the summer months, which correlated with the period of maximum salinity. However, both watering and fertilization failed to alter this different growth pattern. Seed germination similarly shows marked variation. Seeds of *Aster tripolium*, *Puccinellia maritima* and *Spartina anglica*, given uniform pre-treatment and germinated in a controlled environment, showed marked within-species asynchrony in plumule emergence and variation in salinity tolerance (Othman, 1980).

Genetic variation

To what extent may these phenotypic differences be ascribed to genetic differences? That genetic variation and population differentiation occurs in coastal plants is well established since Gregor's (1946) development of the ecotype concept based on studies of *Plantago maritima* populations. In many cases genetic variation has been suggested by the persistence of habit and growth differences when individuals are transferred to the same experimental garden conditions. In other cases reciprocal transplantation experiments have been conducted between low and high marsh populations of a species. If the differences are purely the result of growth in different environments, then the low marsh form could be expected to assume the form of the high marsh plant following transplanting and vice-versa. Such environmental effects appear to explain the differences in form between saltmarsh and rocky shore forms of the brown seaweed *Pelvetia canaliculata* (p. 46). In some species the presence or absence of morphological or physiological markers have been used to demonstrate the existence of genetically different populations. Perhaps the most obvious demonstration of such a marker is in *Aster tripolium*, a species of the Compositae. Individuals of this species on the low marsh, in E. England, rarely produce capitula with any ray florets, whilst individuals on sites of low salinity in the high marsh produce a typical ligulate capitulum with a full complement of ray florets. This floral difference persists in garden culture (Gray *et al.*, 1979).

Population differentiation

Jefferies *et al.* (1979a, 1981) have made detailed studies of populations of *Salicornia europaea* agg. at Stiffkey salt marsh, E. England. On this marsh, as elsewhere in N.W. Europe, the species forms pure stands on mudflats at the lowest levels of the marsh, but is also present in the upper marsh at sites which are reached only by the highest tides and are prone to hypersalination during the summer months. *Salicornia europaea* agg. is one of the few annual plants of the salt marsh. Seed production is very high, apparently, with no viable seed persisting in the soil seed-bank for more than one year. Many seeds die without germinating. Hypersalinity in the high marsh and uprooting by the tides in the lower marsh, together with competition at both sites, result in a very low probability of any one seed reaching maturity. Under these conditions, population differentiation in response to the environment could be expected to be rapid. Seeds of both populations germinate in spring, but those of the upper marsh show little growth until late summer. This may be an adaptation in growth pattern to salinity, since in late summer high tides will reach the upper marsh sites, ameliorating hypersaline conditions. These differences in growth pattern persist on transplantation or when the upper marsh sites are watered and fertilized, suggesting genetic differences. Chromosome numbers did not differ between the two populations, although consistent floral differences demonstrated some genetic differentiation.

The basis of height form differences in *Spartina alterniflora* has attracted much interest. Mooring *et al.* (1971) showed that in culture plants grew to similar heights regardless of whether the seed had been collected from forms which were short or tall in the field. Shea *et al.* (1975) made reciprocal transplants of tall and short forms. Within 17 months short forms transplanted into the area occupied by the tall forms had become morphologically indistinguishable from the latter and vice versa. These results suggested that the phenotypic variations in height form were purely the result of environmental influences on growth and development. Electrophoretic studies have produced conflicting results. Shea *et al.* (1975) failed to detect consistent differences in enzymes, known to show polymorphism, of the two height forms. However, more recent studies of *S. alterniflora* in other locations have revealed small differences between the height forms with respect to the electrophoretic properties of certain enzymes, thus suggesting some genetic differentiation (Anderson and Treshow, 1980).

Field and laboratory experiments have been conducted to identify the environmental factors producing change in height form in a North Carolina marsh. 70% of height form variation could be accounted for by changes in soil drainage (Mendelssohn and Seneca, 1980). Under culture conditions height differences disappeared in anaerobic rooting media, but significant differences persisted in aerobic rooting media, again implying some genetic differentiation (Linthurst, 1980). However, in a long-lived rhizomatous perennial, such as *S. alterniflora*, environmentally-induced differences in a single genotype could persist for a long period. One effect of anaerobiosis may be inhibition of nutrient uptake, since experimental fertilization of the characteristically waterlogged sites of the short form resulted in the conversion to tall form over a 3–4 year period (Valiela *et al.*, 1978). This conversion was not simply a change in the existing short plants but also the result of establishment from seed of new tall-form plants. In these marshes, exposed creek bank sites are typically colonized by seedlings produced by tall-form plants, which have a far greater seed production than short-form plants. In the absence of competition and with a good nutrient supply the seedlings develop into tall plants. Accretion of fine sediment will impede drainage and result in stagnation of the soil water and decreased nutrient supply, the tall plants are weakened and short forms invade the stands vegetatively. Fertilization of areas occupied by short forms reverses this succession (Valiela *et al.*, 1978). The high seed production, invasiveness and fecundity of the tall form in many ways reflect that of an *r*-selected opportunist. However, evidence of significant genetic differentiation is lacking; the only explanation at present being that the rate of environmental change outpaces the rate at which these plants can respond in growth habit.

Other perennial species do, however, show clear genetic differentiation. Gray *et al.* (1979) have shown that population differentiation in *Aster tripolium* occurs in response to altitude within the marsh. In cultivation, high-marsh populations show significant differences from low-marsh populations in germination properties, flowering date, fruit size and longevity. Differences in flowering dates suggest that high- and low-marsh populations in any one marsh would be genetically isolated.

Population interaction

Puccinellia maritima may colonize intertidal muds at the lowest marsh levels and may also be the major component of cover in the middle marsh of salt marshes in W. Europe. It is a long-lived perennial which spreads by stolons and tiller fragments, but will also produce some seed. The species is capable of self-fertilization but is predominantly outbreeding, and in Britain populations are octoploid (Gray and Scott, 1977*a*). This high ploidy will tend to slow down the rate of genetic fixation, i.e. the rate at which full homozygosity is approached (Gray *et al.*, 1979). Measurement of heritable morphological characters suggests that the populations of *Puccinellia maritima* colonizing the low marsh consist of a wide range of genetically distinct clones. Established populations with full ground cover on grazed marshes contain fewer genetically distinct clones, suggesting that genotypes closely adapted to the conditions of increased plant density on the upper marsh are selected from very variable colonizing populations (Gray *et al.*, 1979). Thus, not only is there genetic variation within the individuals of a species on a single salt marsh, but these will interact with each other as well as the environment to bring about change in the genetic makeup of the flora in response to environmental change.

3.4   Interspecific interactions and succession

Primary succession

Just as different individuals of the same species may compete to produce change in the composition of the population with change in the saltmarsh environment, so individuals of different species will interact to produce change in the species composition. Competitive replacement of one species by another in response to environmental change underlies the early ideas on primary succession proposed by Clements (e.g. Colinvaux, 1973). Salt marshes, according to these ideas, are stages in a halosere, i.e. part of a linear change in vegetation from bare tidal flat to the climax vegetation typical of the climatic zone. In such a succession, bare tidal flats are first invaded by colonizing species, such as *Spartina alterniflora* or *Salicornia europaea*. Their presence stabilizes the substrate and promotes accretion,

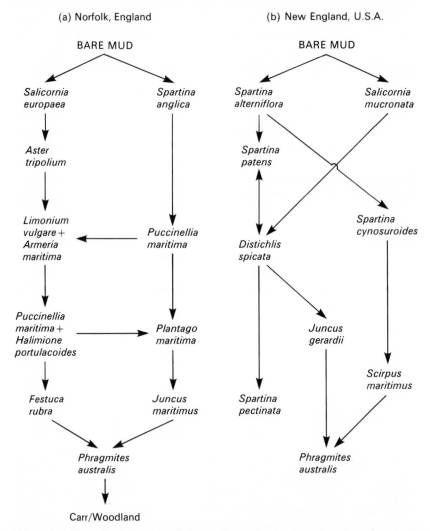

Figure 3.5 Generalized successional changes in the dominant species of vascular plants, following the colonization of bare tidal muds, projected from observed zonations at (a) Norfolk, E. England and (b) New England, U.S.A. (after Chapman, 1974*a*, 1976, 1977).

eventually allowing other species to invade the raised surface. The primary colonizers are lost, due either to their own effects on the physical environment (i.e. altering the marsh surface), or through competitive interaction with other species able to invade the raised surface. This process would continue until the marsh surface is raised above the height of the highest tides and non-halophytic species invade the surface, leading to the establishment of the climax vegetation, e.g. oak woodland in W. Europe.

Although small parts of such a succession can be recognized on many marshes, consistent evidence of a full linear succession of this type is lacking. Few could disagree that such a scheme is an oversimplification of successional changes in saltmarsh vegetation, but opinions clearly differ on the extent to which it is an oversimplification. If an ordered succession does occur, i.e. low marsh is eventually transferred into middle marsh, middle marsh into high marsh, etc., it follows that the altitudinal variation in zonation of vegetation would be a reflection in space of successional changes in time. Chapman (1974a) provides detailed descriptions of successional patterns in vegetation from low to high marsh suggested from observed zonations for each major grouping of world salt marshes (e.g. Fig. 3.5). However, only a few workers have studied changes in the composition of saltmarsh vegetation at fixed sites over several years. The records of Chapman (1959) for the Scolt Head Marshes, E. England, do suggest an ordered change, whilst those of Meesenburg (1971) for the Skallingen, W. Denmark, Richards (1934) for the Dovey estuary, Wales, and Beeftink (1977) for the estuaries of S. Holland, show a far more complex pattern of regression and succession at differing points. A real test of a complete ordered succession is, in any case, precluded by the fact that few coastlines bearing salt marsh appear stable with respect to sea level (section 2.3). On a rising coastline low marsh will eventually be raised to the level of high marsh and above, regardless of whether or not there was net accretion of sediment. Here vegetation change would be expected simply because of a physically driven change in the environment. On a sinking coastline, accretion of sediment will be to some extent counteracted by the overall sinking of the land mass. Accretion rates decrease towards the top of the marsh and succession in the upper marsh would be arrested at the point where sinking and accretion are balanced. This would result in upper marsh being the subclimax vegetation, as hypothesized for Scolt Head, E. England (Chapman, 1974a; Fig. 3.5).

As Ranwell (1972) has observed, "one has only to look at the slumped clods of main marsh level communities doomed to die in the bottom of a creek to realize that the probabilities of any particular square metre of saltmarsh turf taking part in uninterrupted textbook succession may be very low indeed". This probability is even further reduced by other physiographic changes such as cyclical erosion of middle marsh, the smothering of high marsh vegetation by rafts of debris and shingle cheniers driven across the marsh surface (e.g. Greensmith and Tucker, 1966). Further it is clear that some salt marshes may form part of a regressive sequence. As previously noted, some New England marshes overlie remains of pine and broad-leaved forest, indicating a transition from climax vegetation to salt marsh. Thus it would appear that, on a large scale, much vegetational change is a response to physically driven change in saltmarsh physiography and is not primarily the result of changes induced by the vegetation itself. This does not preclude the possibility that the cyclical changes and reversals are short-term fluctuations superimposed on longer term net successional changes of the type proposed by Chapman (1976), at least for marshes on rising coastlines.

Species replacement

Whilst evidence of complete successions on a large scale is lacking, there have been direct observations of partial or complete replacements of one species by another.

Ranwell (1972) records a number of instances where *Spartina anglica* stands are invaded and replaced by other species. At Bridgwater Bay, S.W. England, *Spartina anglica* has invaded bare tidal flats, so forming new low marsh. It is suggested that *S. anglica* retains dominance for about 20 years before it is replaced by species of lower salt tolerance. Three processes were identified in this replacement: suppression of growth by accumulation of its own litter, accretion which created a less saline and drier surface so allowing invasion by *Agropyron pungens* (= *Elymus pycnanthus*), *Scirpus maritimus* and *Phragmites communis* (= *P. australis*), and finally shading by the taller growths of the invading species. It appears that, on this marsh, formation of surfaces suitable for the invading species occurred more rapidly than they could be utilized. Experimental transplants of the invading species, well beyond their natural limits, survived in competition with *S. anglica*.

Scirpus maritimus and *Phragmites communis* are typically found in the high marsh where there are significant inputs of fresh water. In the absence of such conditions these species are unlikely to replace *S. anglica*. About 50 years ago *S. anglica* was planted on bare mudflats of the Stour Estuary, E. England, where it spread to create several hectares of low salt marsh. On the highest parts of this new marsh *S. anglica* has been replaced by *Puccinellia maritima* (Othman, 1980). It is easy to envisage tall growths of *Phragmites communis* shading out the shorter growths of *S. anglica* as suggested by Ranwell (1972), but the same explanation would seem improbable for replacement by the shorter *Puccinellia maritima.* However, examination of leaf demography and canopy structure shows that this is not so simple. *Puccinellia maritima* maintains a canopy throughout the year and significant canopy growth starts in the early spring. Significant shoot growth in *S. anglica* requires much higher temperatures and does not commence until June (Dunn, 1981). Thus in mixed stands *P. maritima* will produce its canopy well before *S. anglica*, so shading the developing shoots (Othman, 1980). Among saltmarsh species, *Spartina* could be particularly susceptible to shading. Plants utilizing the C_4 pathway of photosynthesis, such as *Spartina*, generally show a lower efficiency of light energy conversion under low light conditions than those utilizing the C_3 pathway. *Puccinellia maritima*, *Phragmites communis* and *Scirpus maritimus* belong to the latter group. Replacement of one species by another is not necessarily a gradual change in time, but may occur in bursts. Frost damage to *S. anglica* near its upper limit in Poole Harbour, S. England, opened the marsh surface for colonization by high marsh species (Ranwell, 1972). Invasion of tidal flats by *Spartina anglica* in Europe and *Spartina alterniflora* in N. America does not always lead to the eventual development of a middle or higher marsh community. In some of the older *S. anglica* marshes of S. and E. England and in *S. alterniflora* marshes in North Carolina, bare patches develop in the vegetation due to "die-back" and the area may revert to tidal flat (Goodman *et al.*, 1959; Linthurst, 1980). In these areas accretion of a fine and soft sediment around the *Spartina* has created stagnant conditions and extreme anaerobiosis where plants are weakened and eventually die.

Secondary succession

Although evidence for any complete primary successions is lacking, secondary successions following disturbance to the marsh surface have been demonstrated and are of obvious importance in conservation management. The destruction of vegetation may result from natural causes, but increasingly from man-made alterations. The obvious natural causes in cool temperate and colder zones are unusually heavy frosts and (in warmer climates) fire. Indeed, in the southern U.S.A. periodic fires on the peat surface of the middle and high marsh are believed to maintain the

Spartina patens-dominated areas by preventing the establishment of woody species (Ranwell, 1972).

On the marshes of the Rhine, Meuse and Scheldt estuaries, changes in the composition of the vegetation following severe frosts of 1962–3, waterlogging, and herbicide damage have all been recorded (Beeftink, 1977, 1979). In each case a fairly ordered succession back towards the original vegetation was recorded over a 4–15 year period (e.g. Fig. 3.6). Changes caused by pollution are described in Chapter 7.

Turf-cutting, the commercial removal of strips of high marsh dominated by fine-leaved grasses, has continued for many years on a number of marshes in N.W. Europe (e.g. Gray, 1972). Typically high marsh is mown, sprayed with selective herbicide to remove dicotyledonous species and then the upper 3–4 cm of soil is stripped from the marsh. Secondary succession on resulting bare areas required about five years on salt marshes at Morecambe Bay, N.W. England. At this site and at Bridgwater Bay, S.W. England, *Puccinellia maritima* usually colonized the bare soil first, even if *Festuca rubra* dominated the adjacent uncut areas. *P. maritima* will even invade bare soil at elevations above those in which it

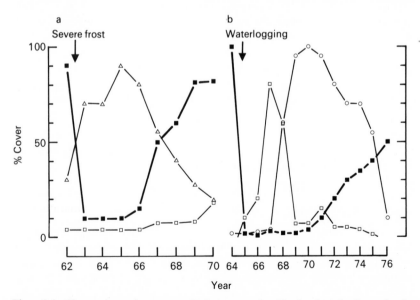

Figure 3.6   Changes in species cover on *Halimione portulacoides* dominated salt marshes in the Netherlands, following (a) a severe frost and (b) a period of severe waterlogging. *Halimione portulacoides* (solid squares), *Aster tripolium* (open squares), *Puccinellia maritima* (circles) and *Artemesia maritima* (triangles); after Beeftink (1977; 1979).

naturally occurs on the same marsh, suggesting that its upper limit is determined by competition with other species rather than edaphic conditions. At these sites it required three years before *F. rubra* covered more ground than *P. maritima* (Gray, 1972). However, if such disturbances are repeated and maintained the marsh will clearly be more prone to erosion and a regression of the vegetation may occur.

Interactions with fauna

Grazing by vertebrates also influences interspecific interactions between plants and the process of succession; wildfowl are particularly important. For example, in the La Pérouse marshes, N. Canada, flocks of snow geese (*Anser caerulescens*) uproot vegetation and puddle the surface of the marsh, these depressions developing a high salinity and allowing colonization by *Triglochin maritima* and *Carex aquatilis*, normally present on the low marsh (Jefferies *et al.*, 1979).

Grazing by domestic animals is also significant. Exclosure experiments on the Skallingen marshes of West Denmark have shown that, in the absence of grazing by sheep, a species-rich saltmarsh community is replaced by pure stands of *Phragmites communis* or *Halimione portulacoides* (A. Jensen, pers. comm.). Grazing is discussed further on pages 83 and 135.

In conclusion, early ideas on a simple linear succession within the salt marsh where each species or sub-community modifies the environment to allow the next stage must be rejected. Changes in the floristic composition are rarely linear, show marked variation between and within sites, show frequent reversals, and are complicated both by phenotypic and genotypic variation within species and by interactions with the fauna and with physiographic change.

CHAPTER FOUR

THE SALTMARSH FAUNA

Salt marshes have a comparatively low faunal diversity because, being transitional habitats between land and sea, they present difficult environments for colonization by animals. Those animals which originate from terrestrial habitats have to cope with the problems of tidal inundation and high salinity. Few species of terrestrial origin can permanently inhabit low marshes, though high marshes, covered only a few times a year by the tide, have a more diverse terrestrial fauna. Species well adapted to saltmarsh habitats are frequently restricted to them. In the low marshes of north-west Germany, Heydemann (1979) found that 75 % of the species are restricted in their natural distribution to salt marshes, compared with only 25 % of species on the high marshes. The extent of tidal incursion is very variable so that poorly adapted populations of terrestrial animals are subject to a high periodic risk of local extinction.

The aquatic component of the saltmarsh fauna, which is of both freshwater and marine origin, must adapt to desiccation and to marked changes in environmental salinity. Most aquatic animals in salt marshes are burrowing forms, escaping the rigours of desiccation at low tide. They are more diverse and more abundant at the seaward edge of the marsh.

The complex creek system and numerous pans within a salt marsh increase the number of species able to survive, but there may be great changes in salinity, from almost fresh water after heavy rain to hypersaline after a prolonged dry spell. At a particular time, within a single marsh, individual pans may vary markedly from one another in salinity. Pans which are basically low in salinity may support a fauna of freshwater origin, including mosquitoes, while pans subject to large salinity changes support only euryhaline species, i.e. those species tolerating marked changes in salinity.

An extensive review of the fauna of tidal marshes is given by Daiber (1982), while estuarine animals in general are described by Green (1968) and Newell (1970).

4.1 Invertebrates of salt marshes

Adaptations to flooding and desiccation

The incoming tide may physically wash many terrestrial animals out of their habitat. Joosse (1976), for example, describes how the springtail *Hypogastrua viatica* can be found drifting in dense masses on the surface of the water after a flood. Heavy mortality occurs, but when the flood recedes a mass migration to the original habitat takes place. Because of poor drainage, many soil-dwelling, air-breathing invertebrates are restricted to the well drained edges of creeks, where tidal erosion may remove whole populations (Treherne and Foster, 1979). The root aphid, *Pemphigus trehernei*, for example, lives on the roots of *Aster tripolium*, but is largely restricted to those plants growing along the edges of creeks. This area has a high percentage of air space in the soil and drains quickly on a falling tide (p. 24). Aphids cannot utilize the main saltmarsh flat because the water-logged soils and prolonged submergence would cause high mortality through asphyxiation (Foster and Treherne, 1975, 1976a).

Many herbivorous species can avoid the dangers of flooding by living within the tissues of halophytes. Some 60 % of saltmarsh Lepidoptera, for example, spend their larval stages within plant tissues (Heydemann, 1979). The tissue-dwelling weevils (Coleoptera, Curculionidae) and gall midges (Diptera, Cecidomyiidae) are also well represented on salt marshes.

Many terrestrial invertebrates have activity rhythms which are synchronized with tidal cycles, so that they can avoid the adverse effects of inundation. The carabid beetle *Dicheirotrichus gustavi*, for example, emerges from its burrow after dark and ranges over the marsh surface. There is an exponential decline in the number of beetles through the night and the few still active at dawn disappear abruptly into the soil, an activity pattern typical of carabid beetles in general (Treherne and Foster, 1977). This behaviour, however, is modified when the marsh is submerged during the night. The first tidal coverage in a particular sequence of spring tides occurred shortly before dawn, when few beetles were active, and the second occurred before dark, when the beetles were below ground, so that the initial tidal coverage exposed very few beetles directly to sea water. The nocturnal activity of the beetles was suppressed by two tidal submergences and it was re-established after an absence of two consecutive tidal sub-mergences. The specific adaptation of *Dicheirotrichus gustavi* to life on the salt marsh is therefore the suppression of nocturnal activity during periods of submerging tides, rather than a circatidal rhythm of activity.

A true circatidal rhythm has recently been described in the springtail

Anurida maritima, which emerges to forage shortly after the retreat of the tide and returns underground at least one hour before the return of the tide (Foster and Moreton, 1981), with an activity rhythm having a period of 12.4 h. During sequences of non-submerging tides the rhythm persisted, as it did in the laboratory, away from tides and under constant light. This enables the springtail, with poor escape reactions, to remain in synchrony during the next period of spring tides and so take avoiding action. The majority of species which have evolved from freshwater ancestors avoid the problems of desiccation by dwelling permanently in salt pans, but these may dry up during the summer. Aquatic insects, such as mosquitoes, with a winged adult stage and rapid larval development, can live a vagrant existence from pan to pan. Other animals, such as copepods, grow rapidly in numbers during good conditions, but have resting stages capable of surviving unfavourable periods of desiccation, which may involve a facultative or obligatory diapause, depending on the species (Champeau, 1979).

Those species derived from the intertidal mudflats burrow into sediments when conditions are unfavourable. Many gastropod molluscs have opercula so that inclement conditions can be avoided by sealing off the shell.

Behavioural and physiological responses to desiccation have been studied in the snail *Melampus bidentatus* (Price and Russell-Hunter, 1975). Under dry conditions, snails congregate under rocks, debris or loose soil, where they remain inactive. The snails suffer a high rate of water loss (6.2% wt h^{-1} at 50% humidity and 20°C), which is inversely proportional to the size of the animal and the relative humidity of the environment. The snails, however, can tolerate desiccation, withstanding water losses amounting to 75–80% of body weight. Water resorption is very rapid, 90% of the water loss being recovered within 40 minutes. *Melampus bidentatus* can survive in the saltmarsh environment because of its behavioural adaptations, its tolerance of desiccation and its ability to rapidly rehydrate when conditions improve.

Respiratory adaptations

Alternate flooding and drying pose respiratory problems for animals living in the salt marsh. It has already been noted how the aphid *Pemphigus trehernei* lives only in those parts of the marsh where air spaces in the soil are large.

Compared with closely related species living in terrestrial habitats, saltmarsh animals tend to have smaller body sizes, which may be related to respiration. For example, in small, saltmarsh-dwelling spiders, such as *Erigone longipalpis*, the epidermis overlying the lung books (the respiratory organs) acts as a tracheal gill, so that the animal can respire when submerged (Heydemann, 1979). Physical gills, such as bubbles of air trapped by epidermal hairs, are widespread in arthropods, while some species show plastron respiration, i.e. an air film is held by hydrofuge hairs in such a way that it cannot be replaced by water and is maintained at a constant volume, enabling an animal to withstand prolonged submersion.

The sediment-dwelling animals of the salt marsh may be exposed to anaerobic conditions for varying periods of time. Anaerobic respiration results in acid end products (commonly lactic acid), which can reduce the pH of the body fluids if they cannot be excreted. No special mechanisms for the excretion of acid end products are likely to occur in animals which habitually live in the low marsh, where anaerobic conditions last only for a short time. In the desiccating conditions of the high marsh, anaerobiosis may be adopted for long periods, when lactic acid excretion occurs. Those animals which extend over the whole marsh, such as littorinid snails, may breathe air, accumulate the end products of anaerobiosis, or excrete these products, depending on the prevailing conditions. The burrow-living lugworms *Arenicola marina* of the upper marsh may have to withstand periods of oxygen depletion of 9–10 hours. The end-products of anaerobiosis are excreted to the surrounding water, though *Arenicola* is also capable of air-breathing (Newell, 1970). Many intertidal animals become quiescent during the period of emersion, so reducing their energy requirements.

A large range of anatomical and behavioural adaptations has evolved in intertidal animals to maximize their rate of oxygen uptake from sea water, and these are detailed by Newell (1970). Many animals have blood pigments which bind with oxygen and increase the effectiveness of the blood in supplying the tissues with oxygen. Haemoglobin is the most common, being characteristic of tubificid worms. The blue haemocyanin is characteristic of many arthropods and molluscs, while haemerythrin (pink when oxygenated) occurs in some polychaetes, sipunculids and priapulids. The green chlorocruorin is present in some polychaetes. These pigments vary in the extent to which they take up and release oxygen at different partial pressures. In the lugworm *Arenicola marina*, the haemoglobin becomes highly saturated with oxygen at very low partial pressures, i.e. it has a high affinity for oxygen, enabling the animal to pick up oxygen at the low levels of availability which prevail in the animal's burrow over long periods of time between the tides. The chlorocruorin in the polychaete

Sabella spallanzanii has a low affinity for oxygen at low oxygen tensions and functions best in highly oxygenated environments. *Sabella* lives sub-tidally and respires through a crown of tentacles extended into currents of well-oxygenated water. The polychaete *Nephthys hombergii* has a haemoglobin with an intermediate affinity for oxygen. Whilst living in similar habitats to *Arenicola*, it may be more capable of anaerobiosis at low tide (Jones, 1972; Calow, 1981).

Environmental conditions strongly influence the affinity of pigments for oxygen. Increasing temperatures reduce the oxygen-carrying capacity of the blood, so limiting the temperature range within which a species can survive. A decreasing salt concentration of the blood also reduces the affinity for oxygen. The oxygen-carrying capacity is also lowered in many species by reduced pH, the so-called Bohr effect. The hydrogen ions pro-duced by respiring tissues influence the dissociation of CO_2 at the tissues in the following way:

$$CO_2 + H_2O \rightleftharpoons H_2CO_3 \rightleftharpoons H^+ + HCO_3^-.$$

A high carbon dioxide concentration causes more oxygen to be given up at any given oxygen pressure and the process facilitates the delivery of additional oxygen to the tissues. Some invertebrates exhibit a reversed Bohr effect, in which reduced pH increases the affinity for oxygen, which may facilitate oxygen saturation at the respiratory surface, while having minimal effect on the delivery of oxygen to the tissues (Calow, 1981). The reversed Bohr effect occurs in animals with low activity, such as molluscs and the king crab *Limulus*, which live in sediments subject to anaerobic respiration, where carbon dioxide levels are likely to be high.

Adaptations to salinity changes

Aquatic invertebrates may be placed into two major groups, osmocon-formers or osmoregulators, with a series of gradations between (Kinne, 1964). Depending on the salinity, some species may function as either conformers or regulators. Osmoconformers maintain their body fluid isosmotic with sea water, so that a change in the concentration of the external medium will result in a corresponding change in the body fluids. Comparatively few animals are isosmotic over a wide range of concentra-tions. Examples are the mussel *Mytilus edulis* and the lugworm *Arenicola marina*, which are common in the Baltic Sea, where they tolerate salt concentrations down to 15% and 30% of normal seawater concentration respectively (Lockwood, 1963). Osmotic regulation in osmoconformers is confined to the cellular level. However, the concentration of individual ions within the body may differ substantially from the external medium, the cellular proteins having a considerable influence on the distribution of ions between the animal and its medium (the Donnan effect).

Osmoregulators maintain their body fluids hyperosmotic to the medium. Such animals encounter two physiological problems. Water flows inwards because of the higher osmotic concentration inside, while solutes flow outwards. Ions are replaced by active transport from the medium, but this process is energetically expensive. To reduce the cost of active transport, the permeability of the body wall is reduced and the concentration gradient between the blood and the external medium is lowered. For example, crabs which live in fresh water, such as *Eriocheir sinensis*, have cuticles of very low permeability. The brackish-water *Carcinus maenas* is slightly more permeable, while the cuticle of the sublittoral swimming crab *Macropipus depurator* is very permeable. Complete impermeability is not possible because of the need to maintain permeable membranes for gas exchange. The ingress of water is removed by excretion, which also results in some loss of ions.

The fall in blood concentration when the medium is diluted decreases the energy expenditure on active transport, but the cells of the body must be able to adapt to the changes, so that the regulatory process overall is divided between the body cells and the mechanisms which maintain the stability of the blood. Species such as *Arenicola* and *Mytilus*, whose cells can tolerate substantial dilution, have blood concentrations very close to those in the external medium. Animals relying on active transport to maintain cellular concentrations maintain blood concentrations between those of the cells and the external medium.

The salinities in saltmarsh pans vary from almost fresh to hypersaline, so that hyporegulation may occur. The brine shrimp *Artemia salina* lives in salt lakes, salinas and salt pans in warm climates and can tolerate salt concentrations ranging from 3–$300 \, g \, l^{-1}$. In dilute sea water, *Artemia* behaves like other brackish-water organisms, maintaining the body fluids hypertonic to the medium. At high external concentrations, the animals lose water to the environment and absorb salts. *Artemia* takes in water, via both the mouth and the anus, and surplus salts are excreted through the first ten pairs of branchiae (Croghan, 1958).

A number of environmental factors, such as temperature, influence the osmoregulatory ability of animals. The life stage is also important. The egg or early larval stages of invertebrates are frequently less tolerant of salinity changes than the more advanced developmental stages, e.g. the crustaceans *Sphaeroma rugicauda* (Marsden, 1973) and *Neomysis integer* (Vlasblom and Elgershuizen, 1977).

The wide range of abilities of insects to tolerate environmental salinity is illustrated in Fig. 4.1. The larva of the mosquito *Aedes detritus*, for example, can tolerate salinities of almost $100 \, g \, l^{-1}$, considerably more than twice normal sea water. Some species, such as *Ephydra riparia* and *Aedes detritus*, maintain an almost stable osmotic concentration in the blood over a wide range of external salinities, while others, such as *Chironomus halophilus* and *C. aprilinus*, can do so over only a limited range of salinities. *Chironomus salinarius* occupies an intermediate position, tolerating a high osmotic concentration in the blood when living in saline waters. The efficient osmoregulators have integuments considerably less permeable than closely related species from fresh waters. The physiological mechanisms involved are reviewed by Foster and Treherne (1976b).

In the majority of studies on the osmoregulatory abilities of invertebrates, the animals are acclimatized to specific salinities. In nature, by contrast, conditions may change very quickly. *Gammarus duebeni*, an amphipod, lives in saltmarsh creeks, in which cyclical changes of salinity

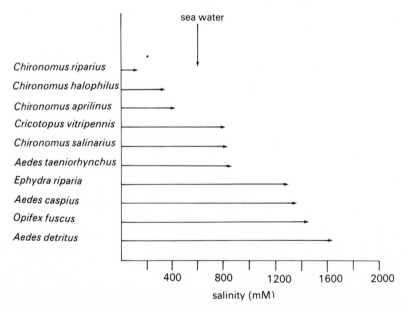

Figure 4.1   Salinity tolerances of dipterous insect larvae from salt marshes, compared with the freshwater-dwelling *Chironomus riparius* (adapted from Foster and Treherne, 1976b).

occur, and in saltmarsh pans, where salinity may be stable for a number of days, but in which salinity conditions alter rapidly after rainfall or tidal inundation. Lockwood and Inman (1979) found that *G. duebeni* maintained its blood concentration within narrow limits when exposed to a 12-hour cycle of salinity changes from fresh water to 50% sea water, with good regulation within a range from fresh water to full sea water. After acclimatization, the blood became almost isotonic with the external medium over the range 50–150% sea water, while much higher salinities could be tolerated, although the animal became inactive.

With a sudden dilution of the external medium from full sea water, there was a rapid fall in the concentration of the blood of *G. duebeni*, but the rate of decline was slowed by an increased uptake of inorganic ions and the production of a urine which was hypotonic to the blood, while the animal's permeability to water was reduced. No significant changes in blood volume were recorded in animals transferred from 100% to 2% sea water. These osmotic capabilities demonstrate how successful has been the adaptation of *Gammarus duebeni* to the severe environment of the salt marsh.

Genetic polymorphism

The saltmarsh environment is highly variable both in space and time, so that we might expect individual animal species to show genetic plasticity to respond to the varying selective pressures within the habitat. However, very little work on the genetics of saltmarsh animals has been conducted. The isopod *Sphaeroma rugicauda* has two patterned and four colour morphs (red, yellow, red-yellow and grey) which can be readily distinguished. Red and yellow are produced by dominant alleles at two closely linked loci, while red-yellow is a combination of the two dominants. Grey is recessive. In most natural populations, yellow is at a low frequency, due to reduced viability. In a saltmarsh population on the Tyne estuary, near Edinburgh, the proportion of yellows was observed to decline over the October–January period during three years (Heath, 1974). In one of these winters, a particularly mild one, the frequency of yellows increased during the period January–March. Laboratory experiments indicated that yellows have a faster growth rate than greys under winter conditions and that large animals survive better than small animals. Initially, yellows survive worse than greys but, when they have grown larger than greys, they have a higher survival.

Heath (1975) found that *Sphaeroma rugicauda* populations in different

estuaries have different genetic constitutions, which suggests that local
conditions such as vegetation and salinity may be very important in controlling morph frequencies. The colour polymorphisms relate to different
physiological tolerances, and the relative advantage of the different forms
changes from place to place and through the year.

4.2 Zonation of invertebrates

With gradients in tidal incursion, desiccation and salinity, zonations of
animals occur across salt marshes, while there may be sharp discon-
tinuities between the fauna of salt marshes and the adjacent intertidal
mudflats. However, zonations of animals within the salt marsh are rarely
clear-cut, because of the mosaic of microhabitats which characterize salt
marshes.

A distinct zonation pattern has been described by Coull *et al.* (1979) in a
community of meiobenthic copepods (Fig. 4.2). On this *Spartina alterniflora* marsh in South Carolina, *Microarthridion littorale* occurred across the
whole transect, from the subtidal to the high marsh. Other species had
more restricted distributions, e.g. *Schizopera knabeni* and *Nitocra lacustris*
occurred only in the high marsh, while *Halectinosoma winonae* and
Pseudobradya pulchella were found only in the low zone. Individual
meiofaunal species varied markedly in numbers both seasonally and
between years, especially on the high marsh (Bell, 1979) and unpredictable

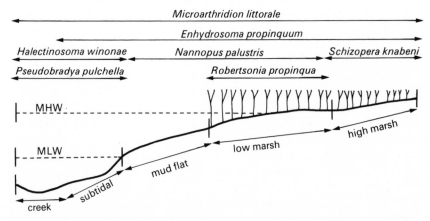

Figure 4.2 Distribution of some meiobenthic copepods along a gradient across a salt
marsh in the south-eastern United States (adapted from Coull *et al.*, 1979).

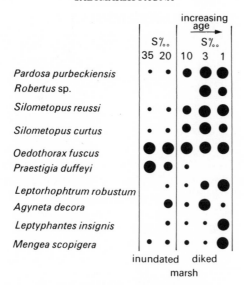

Figure 4.3 Changes in the relative abundance of spiders at different stages in the development of salt marshes in north-west Germany. Soil salinities are shown for each stage in the development (adapted from Heydemann, 1979). Note: $S\% = g\,l^{-1}$.

events, affecting recruitment, are probably the most important influence on the meiofaunal community, as indeed they are on the macrofauna.

Zonations have also been recorded in a number of macrofaunal groups. Heydemann (1979) has studied the zonation of animals associated with plant succession on the north German salt marshes. The plant succession, from pioneer *Salicornia europaea* to a freshwater community including *Leontodon autumnalis*, takes 80–120 years under natural conditions, but with the recent construction of dykes, the sequence is accelerated to between 2–5 years. Fig. 4.3 shows the spiders, the most important arthropod predators on many salt marshes, associated with different plant communities through the succession. In the early salt marsh, dominated by *Puccinella maritima*, only *Oedothorax fuscus* and *Praestigia duffeyi* were common, but the number of spider species and their abundance increased as the soil salinity fell after construction of the dykes. The saltmarsh specialists persisted for a number of years and their mortality was reduced in the absence of flooding. A similar zonation has been recorded in oribatid mites by Luxton (1967*a*, *b*). The mites associated with the high marsh, dominated by the rush *Juncus maritimus*, were essentially terrestrial. Associated with *Festuca rubra* was an intermediate community which could not withstand severe conditions, while those species in the low *Puccinellia maritima* zone of the salt marsh were highly adapted to tidal submergence.

Teal (1959), in Georgia, has examined the zonation of crabs, which was related to their behaviour during a tidal cycle. Three groups of crabs were recognized. The first group (*Eurytium limosum, Panopeus herbsti* and *Sesarma reticulatum*) contained species active only at high tide or in cloudy conditions and they retreated to their burrows at low tide. They inhabit the low marsh. The second group (*Uca pugnax* and *U. minax*) was mainly active at low tide, but also fed at high water and in pans and these species occurred mainly in the intermediate zone of the marsh. The third group of crabs (*Uca pugilator* and *Sesarma cinereum*) was active only at low water and occurred mainly on the high marsh or on the raised edges of creeks in the low marsh. *U. pugilator* retreated to its burrow at high tide, whereas *S. cinereum* climbed vegetation above the high-water level.

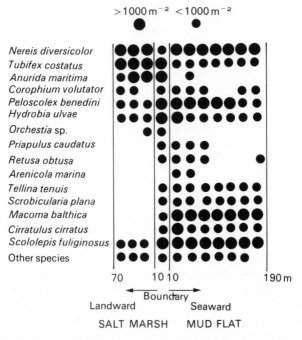

Figure 4.4 Distribution and population density (m^{-2}) of invertebrates recovered from a transect across a salt marsh and mudflat in the Stour estuary, Suffolk, June 1979 (from unpublished data of D. J. Jackson).

An expanding marsh, with a developing vegetation, represents a very different habitat to the rather unstructured mudflat it is replacing. A sharp discontinuity occurs in the macrofauna at the interface between marsh and mudflat, caused not only by the change in structure, microclimate and food supply, but also by the change in predation pressure. D. J. Jackson (unpublished) has sampled along a number of transects across a *Spartina anglica* marsh and into the adjacent mudflat in the River Stour estuary, Suffolk, and a summary of his results is shown in Fig. 4.4. Fifteen species of macrofauna were recorded on the mudflat, compared with only nine species in the salt marsh. Some species were restricted to the mudflat, others were more widespread, but most numerous on the mudflat. The collembolan *Anurida maritima* was largely confined to the transition zone between marsh and mudflat. Although a decrease in diversity correlated with the presence of *Spartina*, there was a strong positive correlation between the biomass of the fauna and the biomass of *Spartina*. The reduced biomass on the mudflat may be due to the heavy predation pressure exerted by wading birds in that area.

4.3 Vertebrates of salt marshes

Fish are restricted to creeks and pools at low tide, but when the salt marsh is inundated they range more widely. Characteristic species in British salt marshes are the sand goby (*Pomatoschistus minutus*) and three-spined stickleback (*Gasterosteus aculeatus*), while juvenile flatfish are also frequent. Sticklebacks often make spectacular migrations to fresh waters to breed and the physiological adaptations to changes in the external osmotic and ionic environment are described by Wootton (1976). In Norfolk salt marshes, the stickleback, small though it is, forms a major component of the diet of the otter (*Lutra lutra*) (Weir and Bannister, 1973).

Because of the danger of flooding, relatively few species of bird use natural salt marshes for breeding. Fuller (1982) divides the breeding community of British salt marshes into six groups.

1. Colonial species, which occupy discrete parts of the salt marsh for breeding, but feed almost exclusively outside the nesting habitat. The common tern (*Sterna hirundo*) and the black-headed gull (*Larus ridibundus*) are the most widespread. Out of a British breeding population of black-headed gulls of 105 000 pairs (Gribble, 1976), 74% breed on coastal marshes, the largest colony being of 18 500 pairs in Hampshire.

2. Widespread non-colonial species which nest throughout the salt marsh, but which show a preference for the slightly higher land bordering creeks. The redshank (*Tringa totanus*) is the characteristic example. Redshank chicks survive the flooding of the low marsh by being able to float (Cadbury, 1973).
3. Middle and high marsh species, which avoid the risk of flooding, e.g. skylark (*Alauda arvensis*), meadow pipit (*Anthus pratensis*), reed bunting (*Emberiza schoeniclus*).
4. Species confined to grazed grasslands on the high marsh, especially lapwing (*Vanellus vanellus*) and yellow wagtail (*Motacilla flava*).
5. Fringe species, associated with the transition between salt marsh and fully terrestrial habitat. This area frequently contains brackish marsh and dykes, where moorhen (*Gallinula chloropus*) and sedge warbler (*Acrocephalus schoenobaenus*) are characteristic.
6. Species which nest elsewhere, but use the salt marsh as a rearing ground for young, especially the shelduck (*Tadorna tadorna*).

Both the species diversity and density of the saltmarsh breeding bird community are low, generally less than 200 pairs km^{-2}. There is a direct relationship between the number of breeding species and the area of salt marsh (Fuller, 1982). On a salt marsh in north-west England, Greenhalgh (1971) recorded fifteen breeding species. Redshanks and skylarks occurred at densities of 22.5 and 18.6 pairs km^{-2} respectively. Apart from the colonial common tern and black-headed gull, all other species had densities of less than 2 pairs km^{-2}.

In the U.S.A., characteristic breeding species of salt marshes are the clapper rail (*Rallus longirostris*), laughing gull (*Larus atricilla*) and several races of "sparrows" (*Ammospiza*, *Melospiza* and *Passerculus*). The difficulty of utilizing salt water limits the numbers of passerines breeding on salt marshes. Of five subspecies of the savannah sparrow (*Passerculus sandwichensis*) in western North America, two are restricted to salt marshes. *P. s. beldingi* drank large quantities of salt water and maintained an almost constant saltwater intake up to 100% sea water, thereafter declining. The better adapted race *P. s. rostratus* reduced its water intake or did not drink for long periods (Bartholomew and Cade, 1963).

The large flocks of waders, so characteristic of the intertidal mudflats, feed but little on salt marshes, though some species (e.g. greenshank *Tringa nebularia*, wood sandpiper *Tringa glareola*) utilize the creeks. The redshank is an exception, feeding on salt marshes at high tide and then following the receding water across the mudflats. Waders do, however, use the salt marsh as a secure roost. Saltmarsh plants, especially members of the Chenopodiaceae and Compositae, produce large crops of seed which attract ducks, feeding at high tide, and passerines, using the exposed salt-marsh (e.g. Olney, 1963, Fuller, 1982). Some passerines, such as the twite (*Carduelis flavirostris*), are almost exclusively saltmarsh birds in winter. Birds of prey are attracted to these feeding flocks.

Grazing ducks and geese are also attracted to salt marsh for feeding and roosting. In Europe the brent goose (*Branta bernicla*) is characteristic, while in the U.S.A. large flocks of snow geese (*Anser caerulescens*) make a significant impact on saltmarsh vegetation by eating roots and rhizomes (Smith and Odum, 1981).

No mammal species can be considered as a saltmarsh specialist. Voles (*Microtus* spp.) and shrews (*Sorex* spp.) are characteristic of the high marsh, but they do not penetrate the low marsh in any numbers. In North America, the muskrat (*Ondatra zibethicus*) is often abundant and it thrives best in those areas with less saline vegetation, such as *Scirpus olneyi* and *S. robusta* (Dozier et al., 1948). The predatory mink (*Mustela vison*) and otter (*Lutra canadensis*) are attracted to salt marshes which have muskrats.

4.4 Feeding

Herbivores make up a small proportion of the total animal biomass on a salt marsh. Halophytic plants have high salt contents, which may vary seasonally, making feeding difficult for many species. The aphid *Macrosiphoniella asteris* tends to select those stems of *Aster tripolium* which have a lower salt content. When feeding on plants growing experimentally in solutions of 0, 15 and 30% sea water, aphids were able to maintain a relatively constant osmotic potential, despite decreases in the osmotic potential of the plant tissues. The aphids quickly died, however, when feeding on plants growing in 60% sea water (Heydemann, 1979). The saltmarsh aphid *Sipha littoralis* is found feeding mainly on *Puccinellia maritima* and *Spartina anglica*, but in laboratory experiments it showed a distinct preference for the glycophyte *Poa annua*, though it does not colonize populations of this species growing adjacent to salt marshes (Heydemann, 1979). This may be due to competition with *Sipha glyceriae*, which does feed naturally on *Poa*.

The majority of herbivorous insects on salt marshes are sapsucking species, such as aphids and other hemipterans, or are chewing species, such as grasshoppers. Within this basic division, however, there are many specialists, feeding on particular plant species or on particular parts of plants.

Grazing vertebrates also show selectivity in feeding habits. Ranwell and Downing (1959), for example, showed that brent geese (*Branta bernicla*), on their arrival on their wintering grounds, fed initially on the beds of seagrass *Zostera* spp., which grow on the mudflats at the lower edge of the salt marsh. This resource was substantially reduced after a month and by midwinter the geese fed chiefly on the alga *Enteromorpha*. Towards the end of winter, the high marsh was exploited, *Puccinellia maritima* and *Aster tripolium* being taken.

The abundance of saltmarsh herbivores may be limited by the nutritional quality of their food. Vince *et al.* (1981) have studied the response of herbivores to the application of fertilizers on a *Spartina alterniflora* marsh in Massachusetts. The herbivore fauna consisted of some 16 species, divided into two feeding groups, sapsuckers (mainly Hemiptera) and chewers (mainly the grasshopper *Conocephalus spartinae*). On both high marsh and low marsh, experimental plots were dosed in spring with a commercial NPK fertilizer at very high (XF), high (HF) and low (LF) application levels, while additional plots were dosed with urea (U), providing nitrogen only at a rate equivalent to the HF dosage. Changes on the plots were compared with controls. The vegetation increased in biomass and, at the high rates of fertilizer addition, also in nitrogen. Figure 4.5 summarizes the effects of the treatments on the herbivorous fauna for the month of August. The herbivorous standing crop increased in all of the treatments, but especially where the nitrogen content also increased. Individual animals grew larger, and survival and fecundity were increased. A change in the structure of the low marsh took place; several species increased in numbers, but the formerly dominant delphacid *Prokelesia marginata* did not, probably due to increased predation by spiders.

Saltmarsh invertebrates of aquatic origin exhibit a number of feeding methods, which are described in detail by Newell (1970). Many molluscs and crustaceans are browsers and scavengers, grazing on the epidermis of living higher plants, on the epiphytic flora growing on the surfaces of plants or sediment and on dead plant and animal material and its associated micro-organisms (Mason, 1974). Deposit-feeders, such as the bivalve *Macoma balthica*, the amphipod *Corophium volutator* and the polychaete *Arenicola marina* extract energy from the organic sediment in which they live. The density of deposit-feeders frequently shows a direct relationship to the quality of the sediment, in terms of nitrogen (Longbottom, 1970). The feeding methods of *Corophium volutator* have been

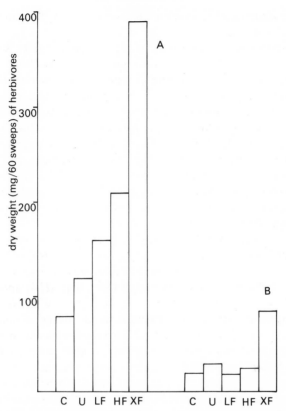

Figure 4.5 Effects of fertilization in spring on the standing crop in August of the herbivores of low marsh (A) and high marsh (B). C = control, U = urea added, LF = low fertilizer, HF = high fertilizer, XF = very high fertilizer. See text for details (adapted from Vince et al., 1981).

studied by Meadows and Reid (1966). *Corophium* lives within a burrow and, using its second antennae, it scrapes organic matter towards itself, depositing it near the entrance to the burrow. The amphipod's pleopods (abdominal limbs) then beat to produce a current which carries the sediment on to the setal filter of the gnathopods (thoracic limbs). This material is then brushed forwards on to the combs of the first gnathopods, which move against one another to sort the material. The maxillipeds (outermost feeding appendages) comb the particles out of the filters on the gnathopods and food is passed forwards to the first maxillipeds and thence to the mandibles, from where it is ingested. As well as feeding from burrows, adult *Corophium* also browse on deposits as they walk across the substratum, while the juveniles, which remain permanently in their burrows, also probably filter-feed.

Many deposit-feeders also function as suspension-feeders (Brafield and Newell, 1961), while filter-feeders often obtain much of their food from bottom deposits. Suspension-feeding is widespread amongst saltmarsh invertebrates and is associated with a general loss of mobility. Newell (1970) divides mechanisms of suspension-feeding into three types. There are animals which produce a mucous sheet, which traps suspended matter and is then eaten, the polychaete *Nereis diversicolor* being a common example. The majority of suspension-feeders employ cilia, whose beating produces currents to carry particles to the animal, where they are sorted and graded. Many polychaetes, gastropods and bivalves feed in this way. A third feeding method is by using setal appendages, a technique adopted by crustaceans, such as barnacles.

Bacteria are very important in the nutrition of deposit-feeders (Newell, 1965; Adams and Angelovic, 1970; Fenchel, 1970). The snail *Hydrobia ulvae* and the bivalve *Macoma balthica* have dense populations in fine substrata, but rather low populations in coarse substrata (Newell, 1965). The fine substrata, because of the greater surface area of their particles, have large populations of bacteria and also a higher organic nitrogen content. From laboratory experiments, Newell observed that the faeces of *Hydrobia* were subjected to a cycle in which bacteria developed on the surface, to be digested by the snail, the voided faeces then being recolonized and the cycle repeated until no more faecal material remained. However, coprophagy has been found to be rare in two species of *Hydrobia* in sediments of small particle size (Levinton and Lopez, 1977; Lopez and Levinton, 1978), though the snails would readily eat faecal pellets which had been broken up. Faecal pellets are only slowly colonized by bacteria so that coprophagous snails took in a diet much poorer in bacteria and diatoms than snails feeding on sediments. The micro-organisms in detritus may be the major source of nutrition for detritivores. Fenchel (1970) showed that the amphipod *Parhyalella whelpheyi* feeds entirely on bacteria, the ingested detritus not being assimilated. This aspect will be detailed in Chapter 6.

Grazing invertebrates can exert a considerable effect on their food supply. The exclusion of the gastropod *Nassarius obsoletus* from a salt marsh resulted in a rapid response by the microflora (Pace *et al.*, 1979). Within three days, the standing crop of both algae and bacteria had increased, while there was also an increase in productivity.

A wide range of predators preys on the herbivores and detritivores within a salt marsh. The role of predators has been examined using cages to exclude them from experimental sites, but there are difficulties in the approach because the enclosure can alter the physical environment as well as exclude the predator. Bell (1980) has examined the interactions between meiofauna and macrofauna in a high salt marsh by excluding the macrofauna from experimental areas. She found that the density of the meiofauna increased sharply in the absence of macrofauna. Copepods of several species increased to a peak within a month, but then declined to control levels. Polychaetes, mainly *Manayunkia aestuarina*, increased more slowly, but showed no signs of a limitation of density. When the cages were reopened to the macrofauna, the densities of meiofauna were sharply reduced. Not all interactions between macrofauna and meiofauna involve predation, however, for the larger animals may provide a more heterogeneous environment, by working the sediments, for the meiofauna.

4.5 Food webs

Building on a knowledge of the diets of animal species living within a salt marsh, a food web can be constructed. Of course, much of the required information is not yet available, but a generalized scheme of the trophic structure of a salt marsh is given in Fig. 4.6. The diet of animals can be studied by direct observation, by examining gut contents or faeces, or by experiments in food preferences. Many saltmarsh species, however, are detritivores, and the origin of their food is difficult to determine, though this information is essential in constructing energy budgets for salt marshes.

Recently, the ratios of the isotopes ^{13}C and ^{12}C have been examined in tissues in an attempt to elucidate food webs. The ^{13}C ratio in animal tissues reflects the average intake of this isotope in the diet over extended periods of time (De Niro and Epstein, 1978). C_4 plants differ from C_3 plants in lacking photorespiration and this gives them a greater potential for growth at high temperatures and light intensities (page 55). The ^{13}C values enable C_3 and C_4 plants to be readily separated, because, although all plants distinguish against the heavy ^{13}C isotope, C_3 plants discriminate more than C_4 plants, giving $^{13}C/^{12}C$ ratios characteristic of each group. C_4 vascular plants have isotopic ratios ($\delta^{13}C$ values) ranging from -9 to $-19\%_{oo}$, negative because samples are more depleted in their ^{13}C composition than the standard used in the analysis. C_3 plants, however, have values ranging from -24 to $-34\%_{oo}$, while the range for algae is intermediate, from -12 to $-23\%_{oo}$ (Haines 1976a, b; Thayer et al., 1978). The isotopes

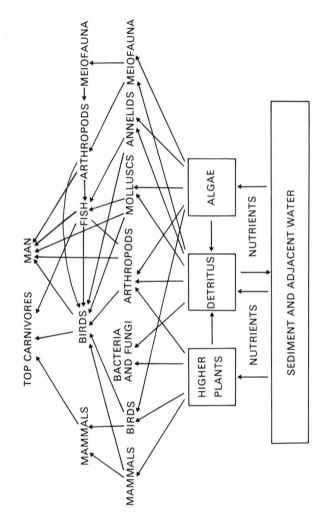

Figure 4.6　Simplified food web on a salt marsh.

are determined using a mass spectrometer. The method is most useful when no more than two distinct sources of carbon, with significantly different $\delta^{13}C$ values, are present, though categories can be combined in more diverse situations. There are few C_4 plants in temperate salt marshes, while in Britain *Spartina* is the only naturally occurring higher plant of any significance with C_4 photosynthesis. It is not possible to determine whether an animal is feeding directly on a particular source, or indirectly by ingesting bacteria which have obtained their carbon from that source (Montague *et al.*, 1981).

The grazers eating live *Spartina alterniflora* tissue on Sapelo Island salt marsh, Georgia, had $\delta^{13}C$ values very close to that of their food plant (Pfeiffer and Wiegert, 1981) and this has also been found with the sap-sucking bug *Philaenus spumarius* feeding on *Spartina anglica* in an Essex salt marsh (D. J. Jackson, pers. comm.). Detritivores show a greater variation (Montague *et al.*, 1981), mirroring the $\delta^{13}C$ values of the vascular plants living close by. Fiddler crabs, for instance, were found to show $\delta^{13}C$ values skewed in the direction of benthic algae, which form a significant part of their diet. Those fiddler crabs collected from small stands of C_3 plants within the *Spartina* marsh in Georgia had higher $\delta^{13}C$ values than could be explained by a diet of benthic algae and C_3 plant detritus, suggesting that they obtained significant *Spartina* carbon by tidal transport or by excursions out of the C_3 stand (Montague *et al.*, 1981). The $\delta^{13}C$ values in filter-feeding molluscs suggested that they fed on algae and chemoauto-trophic micro-organisms, very little of their carbon being derived directly or indirectly from *Spartina* detritus. The use of stable carbon isotopes is a valuable technique in elucidating carbon flow within a salt marsh, but as the isotopic composition of macroconsumers is influenced by a variety of factors, the technique must be used with care.

A knowledge of diets and food webs forms the basis of studies of energy flow through ecosystems and these will be described for salt marshes in Chapter 6.

CHAPTER FIVE

PRIMARY PRODUCTION IN
SALT MARSHES

Within the saltmarsh ecosystem energy and carbon utilized by hetero-
trophs may be derived either from material imported with the tides or from
plant material produced *in situ*. The balance between these two processes
will clearly vary greatly with local conditions. Carbon budget studies
suggest that net primary production, i.e. the plant production *in situ*, is the
major source (e.g. Teal, 1962; Houghton and Woodwell, 1980; Woodwell
et al., 1979; Wiegert, 1979).

Salt marshes are reputedly "among the most productive communities
known" (Whittaker, 1975). Similar statements may be found in many other
introductory texts on ecology. Ostensibly there is a great volume of
information to support this view. However, close examination reveals that
the bulk of this information relies on assumptions which are clearly of
doubtful validity. In view of the importance of methodological limitations
to primary production measurement in salt marshes, this chapter will not
only report some of the findings of these studies, but also outline the
methods utilized and indicate their limitations.

5.1 Biomass

Plant biomass (W) may be defined as the amount of living plant material
contained within and above a unit of ground surface area for a given point
in time. Both biomass and net primary production may be expressed in
terms of any conserved quantity, i.e. energy, carbon or dry weight of
organic material, the last being the most commonly used because of the
ease with which it may be measured. In many studies of saltmarsh production, biomass has been equated with net primary production, although
from a theoretical viewpoint the two are quite distinct (Long and Woolhouse, 1979). Biomass is the integral of past net primary production less all
losses, i.e. it is the quantity present at a fixed point in time, whilst net
primary production is a rate. The relationship between biomass and net
primary production is complex and as yet largely unpredictable.

However, in the context of ecosystem management, biomass is of importance, since it is the amount of plant material available to other producer levels at any given point in time. For example, the high primary productivity of a stand of saltmarsh vegetation will have little significance to an over-wintering flock of geese if all of the production has decomposed or has been washed from the marsh by the date of the migrants' arrival. In this case it is the winter biomass and not the net primary production that is of direct importance.

Shoot or above-ground biomass (W_s) is commonly determined in salt marsh, as in grasslands, by clipping the vegetation at ground level from quadrats selected by a randomized design. The vegetation is then dried to a constant weight. Inorganic contents of saltmarsh vegetation can account for 50% or more of the dry weight (e.g. Hoffnagle, 1980; Hussey and Long, 1982) and thus it is more meaningful to express biomass in terms of ash-free dry weight, calculated after burning the dried samples at 500°C. Since biomass, by definition, implies living tissue, dead shoot material has to be separated from the living. This is extremely time-consuming and limits the number of samples and frequency with which samples may be taken. However, Jensen (1980) has demonstrated a remote sensing technique, based on the infra-red reflectance of live shoots, for the determination of biomass *in situ* in a salt marsh, which would greatly decrease the time necessary for sampling.

Table 5.1 illustrates the range of plant biomass values for some contrasting locations and species (for more detailed compilations see Turner, 1976; Reimold, 1977; Hussey and Long, 1982). Maximum shoot biomass, the highest biomass recorded within a year, ranges from 145 g m^{-2} for a *Puccinellia phryganodes*-dominated salt marsh in Arctic Canada (Jefferies, 1977) to 3018 g m^{-2} for pure stands of *Spartina alterniflora* in a salt marsh in Georgia, U.S.A. (Odum and Fanning, 1973). A latitudinal gradient of maximum biomass has been suggested for *Spartina alterniflora* on the east coasts of N. America (Table 5.2). However, variation within a locality or even the same marsh appears often to exceed any latitudinal differences. As discussed earlier (p. 61) two height forms of *S. alterniflora* are commonly found and the maximum biomass of the tall form is typically 3–4 times that of the short form within the same salt marsh (see Table 5.1).

Maximum shoot biomass has been determined for over 200 stands of saltmarsh vegetation (e.g. Turner, 1976; O'Keefe, 1972), although more than half of this work concerns the *Spartina alterniflora* marshes of the eastern U.S.A. Below-ground biomass in salt marshes has been, until very recently, a neglected subject. Turner (1976), in reviewing the literature on saltmarsh primary production, reported 140 estimates of above-ground biomass but only three estimates of below-ground biomass. No doubt the paucity of information on this topic reflects the many difficulties involved in extracting root systems and identifying live material. Below-ground biomass is determined by extracting soil cores and then washing out the

Table 5.1 Above-ground plant biomasses and masses of dead matter per unit of salt marsh ground area $(g\,m^{-2})$. Mean values are averages for the whole year and maximum values are the highest values recorded within a year. L = low marsh, M = middle marsh, H = high marsh and $-$ = no data. After Hussey and Long (1982), Burg *et al.* (1980), Smith *et al.* (1980), Ruber *et al.* (1981), and Jacobsen and Kristensen (pers. comm.).

Location	Level	Species	Biomass Mean	Max.	Dead Mean	Max.
Netherlands	H	*Agropyron pungens*	528	768	435	544
Netherlands	M	*Puccinellia maritima*	341	576	192	400
Netherlands	M	*Puccinellia maritima*	252	463	84	277
Netherlands	M	*Puccinellia maritima*	153	283	63	169
England	M	*Puccinellia maritima*	328	495	869	1260
Arctic Canada	L	*Puccinellia phryganodes*	—	145	—	—
Netherlands	H	*Juncus gerardii*	197	346	129	262
Delaware, U.S.A.	H	*Juncus gerardii*	—	560	462	748
Washington, U.S.A.	M	*Carex lyngbei*	371	1180	—	270
Washington, U.S.A.	M	*Distichlis spicata*	266	920	—	380
Nova Scotia, Canada	L	*Spartina alterniflora*	190	704	40	160
Massachusetts, U.S.A.	L	*Spartina alterniflora*	406	1190	124	318
Massachusetts, U.S.A.	M	*Spartina alterniflora*	209	408	307	378
Georgia, U.S.A.	L	*Spartina alterniflora*	—	3018	—	—
Denmark	L	*Spartina anglica*	100	243	—	—
N.W. England	L	*Spartina anglica*	—	1680	—	—
S.E. England	L	*Spartina anglica*	198	341	192	200

Table 5.2 Variation in maximum shoot biomass for *Spartina alterniflora* marshes along the east coast of the U.S.A. (after Turner, 1976).

Location	*n*	$g\,dwt\,m^{-2}$ mean	s.d.
Texas	4	756	237
N. Florida	4	701	114
Louisiana	5	643	186
Georgia	1	762	—
N. Carolina	3	497	86
Virginia/Maryland	4	431	68
New England	2	418	139
All sites	23	620	177

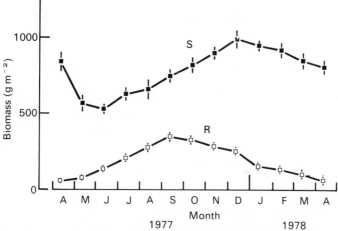

Figure 5.1   Biomass of *Spartina anglica* shoots (S) and roots with rhizomes (R) over twelve months on a salt marsh on the Stour Estuary, E. England (after Dunn, 1981).

roots and rhizomes. Live material may be separated from dead after vital staining, though this again is tedious and very time-consuming. Root biomass in a *Spartina anglica* marsh in E. England accounted for more than 60% of the total in all months (Fig. 5.1). In each of four contrasting saltmarsh communities, below-ground biomass accounted for more than half of the total (Table 5.3). Cammen *et al.* (1974) and Williams (1972) reported below-ground biomasses amounting to 75% of the total for two *S. alterniflora* marshes in North Carolina, whilst in a Louisiana *S. alterniflora* marsh below-ground biomass amounted to more than 90% of the total (Turner, 1976). Even these apparent large proportions are probably underestimates, since the techniques of soil washing and sorting have been shown to underestimate the absolute quantity by 20–50% (Johnen and Sauerbeck, 1977; Sauerbeck and Johnen, 1977).

Table 5.3   Below-ground biomass, mean and maximum values (g dwt m^{-2}), and the ratio of above-ground to below-ground biomass. After Hussey and Long (1982); Ruber *et al.* (1981); and Hoffnagle (1980).

		Mean	Max.	Ratio
Puccinellia maritima	E. England	364	468	0.90
Spartina anglica	E. England	810	1010	0.27
Spartina alterniflora	Massachusetts, U.S.A.	750	1000	0.43
Scirpus validus[a]	Washington, U.S.A.	8587	13 825	0.05

[a] Includes other species.

Multiplication of the maximum or end of season above-ground biomass by the areas of salt marsh suggests very large resources of plant material for other trophic levels. The $200 \, \text{km}^2$ of salt marsh in Georgia may contain a late summer maximum of between 4.2×10^5 and 6.5×10^5 tonnes, whilst in England the $50 \, \text{km}^2$ of salt marsh on the Essex coast would contain a peak in the region of 2.5×10^4 tonnes, with an additional 6.3×10^4 tonnes of dead shoots (calculated from Odum and Fanning, 1973; Wiegert, 1979; Hussey and Long, 1982). These figures would be at least doubled if below-ground biomass was also considered. Such extrapolations should only be regarded as indications of the maxima attained within the region since practical constraints invariably mean that the study sites are subjectively chosen and are not a truly random sample of the salt marsh within a region. Even within an area of marsh flat and at the same tidal level considerable variation in biomass over short distances may be found. Biomass within quadrats placed randomly within a monotypic stand of *Spartina anglica* varied from $162 \, \text{g m}^{-2}$ to $667 \, \text{g m}^{-2}$ (Dunn, 1981). In addition, there may be significant year-to-year variation within the same area of marsh. Maximum biomass of a stand of *Puccinellia maritima*-dominated middle marsh was $330 \, \text{g m}^{-2}$ in 1977, but $285 \, \text{g m}^{-2}$ in 1978, a statistically significant difference (Hussey, 1980; Hussey and Long, 1982).

Many factors, edaphic, climatic and genetic, will clearly underlie this variation. As might be expected from the poor nitrogen supply noted for at least some saltmarsh soils (p. 35), fertilization with inorganic forms of nitrogen invariably results in a significantly increased biomass (e.g. Valiela and Teal, 1974; Patrick and DeLaune, 1976; Smith *et al.*, 1980; Othman, 1980). Broome *et al.* (1975*b*) showed that N fertilization increased the shoot biomass of *S. alterniflora*. Additions of phosphate fertilizers had no significant effect, but showed a significant synergistic effect if combined with N fertilization. A similar synergistic interaction of the effects of N and P fertilization on *S. anglica* in E. England was reported by Othman (1980). A range of N fertilizer application rates on North Carolina *S. alterniflora* marshes showed a linear increase in shoot biomass with application rate, but only a small increase in below-ground biomass (Fig. 5.2). Morris (1982) similarly showed, under controlled environment culture, that increase in supply of inorganic nitrogen to *S. alterniflora* plants resulted in an increased production of shoot and rhizome material, but had no significant effect on root production. The increased biomass observed in the field may not simply be a result of increased production, but also of decreased mortality. Othman (1980) showed that a combined application of $5 \, \text{g (N)} \, \text{m}^{-2}$ and $1.5 \, \text{g (P)} \, \text{m}^{-2}$ in a *Spartina anglica* marsh extended

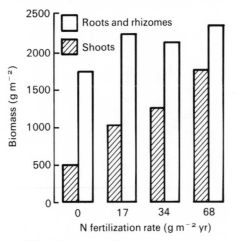

Figure 5.2 The effect of N fertilization on the biomass of *Spartina alterniflora* on a North Carolina, U.S.A., salt marsh (after Broome *et al.*, 1975*b*).

mean leaf longevity from 15 weeks in control plots to 27 weeks in the fertilized plots. A similar effect was observed during experimental fertilization of stands of *Puccinellia maritima*.

5.2 Net primary production

The net primary production (P_n) of the vegetation covering a unit area of ground is the mass, or energy, incorporated by photosynthesis (gross primary production) less that respired during a given time interval (Milner and Hughes, 1968). That is:

$$P_n = P_g - R \tag{5.1}$$

where P_n = net primary production
P_g = gross primary production
R = respiration

Both P_g and R can in theory be determined by measurement of CO_2 fluxes, although in practice it is technically very difficult to measure in any field situation and especially so in a tidal marsh. Since P_n denotes a gain of material by the plant community, it may also be determined from the sum of the changes in plant biomass (ΔW) and all losses over a given time interval (Fig. 5.3). Net primary production may then be redefined:

$$P_n = \Delta W + L + G + E \tag{5.2}$$

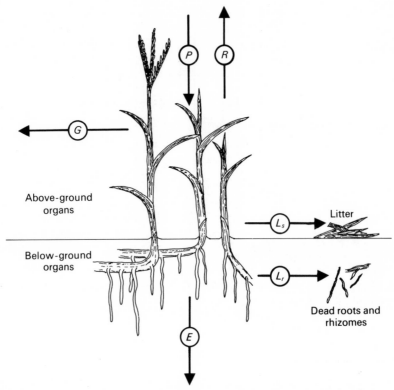

Figure 5.3 Diagram illustrating carbon exchanges between saltmarsh vascular plants and their environment. Stand photosynthesis or gross primary production (P_g), respiration (R), grazing (G), shoot death (L_s), root and rhizome death (L_r), and root exudation (E).

> where ΔW = change in biomass
> L = losses by death or shedding
> G = loss to grazers, i.e. predation
> E = loss through root exudation

Methods of determining biomass at fixed points in time have already been outlined. Losses of shoot material may be determined directly by mapping and marking the shoots contained within permanently positioned quadrats at regular intervals, so that death or loss of individual leaves or stems may be measured. The weights of material lost can then be derived from the regression of weight on a non-destructive measure such as leaf length or area. The relationship between these variables is established from parallel destructively harvested samples. Alternatively, loss may be determined by measuring the change in the amount of dead material and accounting for the rates of loss of this material. In most communities the only significant loss of dead material would be through decomposition, including consumption by macro-invertebrates. In salt marsh an added complication is tidal import and export of dead vegetation:

$$L = \Delta W_d + D + T_e + T_i \qquad (5.3)$$

where ΔW_d = change in dead vegetation
D = loss due to decomposition
T_e = tidal export of material
T_i = tidal import of material

Both direct and indirect techniques of estimating loss require repeated and regular measurement throughout the year. Probably as a result of the difficulties and time required to undertake such a study, many attempts to estimate net primary production in salt marshes have tried to extrapolate a value from measured biomass, making specific assumptions. These techniques have been reviewed by Linthurst and Reimold (1978a) and are outlined in Table 5.4.

The vast majority ($> 90\%$) of P_n estimates reviewed by Turner (1976) were based on extrapolation from the maximum biomass, i.e. the sum of biomass and the weight of dead material (methods 1–3, Table 5.4). These methods, originally developed for annual grasses, assume that no material is lost before the maximum biomass is achieved and that no growth occurs after the maximum has been reached. Dunn (1981), in a study of shoot and leaf demography in a *Spartina anglica* marsh, reported significant losses through death in every month of the year. Methods 4 and 5 (Table 5.4) have been devised to alleviate these limitations, but still fail to account for new shoot growth during periods of high mortality. Linthurst and Reimold (1978) showed that values of P_n extrapolated by these methods could vary 3–4 times between methods, the relative differences between the methods changing both with species and location. Table 5.5 compares P_n determined by actual measurement of the components of eqn. 5.2 with estimates calculated by the extrapolation methods (Table 5.4). Both for a middle marsh community dominated by *Puccinellia maritima* and a low marsh community dominated by *Spartina anglica*, underestimation of P_n is apparent for all of the extrapolation methods.

Yet a further limitation to many data for saltmarsh primary production, as with biomass, is the failure to take account of below-ground production, most previous studies being of above-ground production (AP_n) only. In the

Table 5.4   Methods used to estimate P_n in salt marshes by extrapolation from biomass measurements. $W_{1(max)}$ = Maximum biomass recorded during the year, $W_{1(min)}$ = Minimum biomass recorded during the year, W_d = Mass of dead plant material, Δ = Net change in a quantity between two sampling dates, P_n^i = Primary production between two sampling dates, P_n = Annual primary production.

1. Maximum live dry weight

$$P_n = W_{1(max)}$$

Assumptions:
    (i) No carry-over of biomass from one year to the next.
    (ii) No death occurs before the maximum biomass is gained.

2. Maximum standing crop

$$P_n = W_{1(max)} + W_d$$

Assumptions:
    (i) No carry-over of either biomass or dead material from one year to the next.
    (ii) Dead material does not decompose before the maximum biomass is obtained.

3. Maximum-minimum

$$P_n = W_{1(max)} - W_{1(min)}$$

Assumptions:
    (i) As for method 1, but accounts for any carry-over of material between years.

4. International Biological Programme (Milner and Hughes, 1968)

$$P_n = \Sigma(\Delta W_1) \qquad \text{(negative } \Delta W_1 \text{ is taken as zero)}$$

Assumptions:
    (i) Death and growth do not occur simultaneously.
    (ii) P_n is never negative.

5. Smalley's method (Linthurst and Reimold, 1978a)
P_n^i for any given interval is determined according to the following conditions.

IF $W_1 > 0$ and $W_d > 0$	THEN	$P_n^i = W_1 + W_d$
IF $W_1 < 0$ and $(W_1 + W_d) > 0$	THEN	$P_n^i = W_1 + W_d$
IF $W_1 > 0$ and $W_d < 0$	THEN	$P_n^i = W_1$
IF $(W_1 + W_d) < 0$	THEN	$P_n^i = 0$

$$P_n = \Sigma P_n^i$$

absence of a simultaneous estimate of below-ground production (BP_n), it is impossible to separate production of new material by photosynthetic assimilation from redistribution of existing material between above- and below-ground parts of the plant. No study, to date, has taken account of organic material excreted into the rhizosphere (E of eqn. 5.2). Studies of arable crops show that this loss may amount to as much as 50% of the

Table 5.5 Estimates of net annual primary production according to the extrapolation methods of table 5.4 compared with evaluations according to eqn. 5.2.

Species	Spartina anglica	Puccinellia maritima	Spartina patens	Juncus gerardii
Location	E. England[1]	E. England[2]	Georgia[3]	Maine[3]
Method				
1. Max. live dry wt.	341	310	942	244
2. Max. standing crop	506	800	—	—
3. Max.-Min.	283	254	—	—
4. IBP method	283	—	705	244
5. Smalley's method	271	420	1674	562
6. Eqn. 5.2[b]	702[a]	807	3925	616

[1] Dunn (1981),[2] Hussey (1980), [3]Linthurst and Reimold (1978a).
[a] Losses measured by direct observation of permanent quadrats.
[b] None of these studies takes account of root exudation.

total carbon assimilated (Bowen, 1980). If similar losses occur on salt marshes then even the most detailed estimates of P_n may in fact be serious underestimates.

From the limited data available (e.g. Table 5.6) below-ground production would appear to be substantial, although as may be expected in communities dominated by perennating herbs, the indicated turnover of below-ground organs is less than that of the above-ground. From the very

Table 5.6 Net primary production above-ground (AP_n) and below-ground (BP_n), as measured by evaluation of eqn. 5.2 for different saltmarsh communities. Quantities are ash-free dry weights (g m^{-2} y^{-1}). G = losses through grazing, T_s = turnover of above-ground biomass per year, T_r = turnover of below-ground biomass per year.

Species	Location	Level	AP_n	T_s	G	BP_n	T_r
Spartina alterniflora (Wiegert, 1979)	Georgia	L	4251	—	31	2405	—
Spartina alterniflora (Wiegert, 1979)	Georgia	M	1520	—	—	2294	—
Spartina alterniflora (Woodwell et al., 1979)	New York	L+M	1596	1.7	—	638	—
Spartina alterniflora (Linthurst and Reimold, 1978a)	Maine	L	1602	3.7	—	—	—
Spartina anglica (Dunn, 1981)	E. England	L	702	2.1	0	649	0.65
Puccinellia maritima (Hussey, 1980)	E. England	M	807	2.6	4	606	1.3
Scirpus maritimus (Hoffnagle, 1981)	Washington	M	1200	1.5	82	—	—

Table 5.7 Gross primary production (P_g), respiration (R), and net primary production (P_n), based on gas exchange measurements. All figures represent organic dry weights.

Species	Location	P_g	R/P_g	R	P_n
Spartina alterniflora (Houghton and Woodwell, 1980)[a,b]	New York	4490	0.60	2700	1790
Spartina patens (Drake and Read, 1981)	Maryland	1760	0.58	1020	740
Spartina anglica (Dunn, 1981)[a]	E. England	4500	0.69	3120	702

Calculated from authors' data assuming [a] a C content for the organic matter of 0.39 and [b] correcting for unvegetated area.

limited information based on techniques which attempt to actually evaluate the components of eqn. 5.2, P_n is remarkably high in the Georgia *S. alterniflora* salt marshes, at over $60\,t\,ha^{-1}$ for the low marsh. This corresponds with the best dry-matter yields for crops in the same climatic region. Further north, P_n for the two marshes in E. England (Table 5.6), is relatively high at about $15\,t\,ha^{-1}$, but only half of this is above-ground. However, fertilization experiments suggest that the above-ground P_n of $7\,t\,ha^{-1}$ for *S. anglica* may be well below the potential in England (Othman, 1980).

5.3 Gross primary production

Net primary production is the net balance between the photosynthetic assimilation, or gross primary production (P_g), and respiration (R). Thus, if we wish to seek any physiological understanding of the basis of variation in net primary production, P_g and R must be measured and their responses to environmental variation established (Long and Woolhouse, 1979). P_g may be determined either directly by measuring CO_2 uptake by the plants or indirectly by measuring respiratory losses (R) and then adding these to estimates of P_n, measured by the methods outlined in the previous section. In view of the many sources of error involved in the measurement of P_n it would seem unwise to add the further error of respiration measurement in attempts to estimate P_g. For this reason the few studies of saltmarsh P_g have utilized the direct method of measuring CO_2 assimilation. P_g may then be recalculated in terms of organic material from measured carbon contents of the plants concerned.

Three procedures for estimating P_g by measurement of CO_2 assimilation may be identified. Photosynthetic CO_2 assimilation by individual leaves within the canopy may be determined by measurement, with an infra-red gas analyser, of CO_2 depletion within an enclosing chamber or by measurement of $^{14}CO_2$ uptake (Giurgevich and Dunn, 1978; Long and Incoll, 1979; Long, 1981). Assimilation of CO_2 by the whole canopy may then be extrapolated from a knowledge of canopy architecture. Alternatively, a small area of marsh may be enclosed in a large transparent enclosure and CO_2 fluxes determined by infra-red gas analysis (Drake and Read, 1981). In this method it is essential that the microclimate within the enclosure is controlled to mimic that of the adjacent unenclosed vegetation as closely as possible. A third procedure is to estimate the CO_2 assimilation of the community without enclosure and so avoid the possible effects that enclosure may have on microclimate. This may be achieved by measurement of the CO_2 gradients above the surface concurrently with air movement. Basically, as the vegetation assimilates CO_2 so the CO_2 concentration in the air immediately above and surrounding the plants will decrease, the effect diminishing with height above the vegetation. The change in CO_2 concentration at different heights above the surface will be determined by the rate of CO_2 assimilation by the vegetation and the rate at which air movements replenish the CO_2. CO_2 concentration profiles are most marked above vegetation of even height, such as fields of arable crops, but also many salt marshes. CO_2 concentration and wind speed at different heights above the surface are determined by erecting a mast within the vegetation and sampling air at different heights with simultaneous measurement of windspeed (for an explanation of theory and practice, see Biscoe et al., 1975a,b). If soil respiration is measured simultaneously then CO_2 exchange by the vegetation may be separated from exchange for the community as a whole. Thus, a complete and continuous picture of the exchanges of C between a salt marsh and the atmosphere, hour by hour, may be obtained. CO_2 fluxes determined by this method for the whole saltmarsh community at Flax Pond, New York, are illustrated in Fig. 5.4, describing all exchanges over three consecutive days.

Table 5.7 summarizes measurements of saltmarsh P_g made by all of the three approaches outlined above. Although each estimate was based on a different procedure, all suggest that respiratory losses account for 60–70% of P_g. This high respiratory loss is not surprising when the costs of maintaining a very high proportion of below-ground tissue are considered (Table 5.3). In addition, mechanisms of salt exclusion and excretion (p. 53), soil re-oxidation (p. 58) and symbiotic nitrogen fixation (Boyle and Patriquin, 1981) require considerable respiratory energy. In summary, the

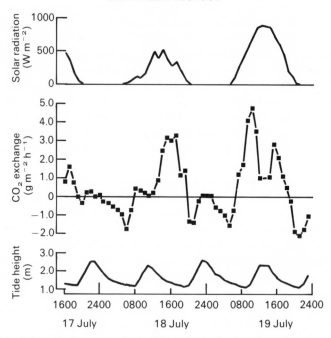

Figure 5.4 Solar radiation, atmospheric CO_2 exchange by the saltmarsh community, and tide height over 3 days on the Flax Pond salt marsh, New York, U.S.A. (after Houghton and Woodwell, 1980).

limited data on P_g suggest that at least the *Spartina* spp. of the salt marsh are capable of very high rates of CO_2 assimilation. Equally, however, they appear to require large amounts of assimilated C for respiratory processes so that any factor which marginally decreases P_g could dramatically lower P_n, turning a highly productive community into a rapidly degenerating one.

5.4   Algal production

This chapter has considered so far only the higher plants of the salt marsh. The primary production of algae within salt marshes has attracted relatively little research effort, even though Teal (1962) suggested that it could amount to 20% of the total primary production of a Georgia saltmarsh ecosystem.

The net primary production (P_n) of the saltmarsh macroalgae, such as the fucoids, has been measured by the procedures outlined already for the shoots of higher plants (Woodwell *et al.*, 1979). Production by benthic microalgae and phytoplankton in the waters of the salt marsh have been measured by ^{14}C assimilation (e.g. Moll, 1977).

Wiegert (1979) reported algal production in a Georgia *S. alterniflora* marsh of $180 \, g \, C \, m^{-2} \, y^{-1}$ (*c.* $420 \, g$ (dry-matter) $m^{-2} \, y^{-1}$). Woodwell *et al.* (1979) in a summary of the measurements made in the Flax Pond salt marsh, New York, estimated a total P_n of $274 \, g \, m^{-2} \, y^{-1}$ or 21% of total P_n. The marsh fucoids accounted for the bulk of this production, $150 \, g \, m^{-2} \, y^{-1}$. Maximum production for the fucoids was between late autumn and early spring when higher plant production was least. The remainder of the algal production at Flax Pond was accounted for by epiphytes ($60 \, g \, m^{-2} \, y^{-1}$), epibenthos ($40 \, g \, m^{-2} \, y^{-1}$) and phytoplankton ($23 \, g \, m^{-2} \, y^{-1}$). The contribution of epibenthic algae thus amounted to 5% of the total P_n of the marsh. However, for *S. alterniflora* marshes in North Carolina, Gallagher and Daiber (1974) and Van Raalte *et al.* (1976) both estimated P_n for epibenthic algae at $20-25 \%$ of the marsh total, although both studies showed a decrease in epibenthos production in areas of high *S. alterniflora* above-ground biomass.

The limited information available suggests a net productivity by the algae of about 20% of the total. However, this production is spatially and temporally separate from that of the higher plants, being largely limited to unvegetated areas such as salt pans and creek banks or occurring on the marsh flat, when the shoots of higher plants have died back in the late autumn.

In conclusion, salt marshes may indeed be highly productive habitats as was suggested in earlier accounts (p. 90). If this view is to be accurately quantified for region, species and environmental conditions, many more detailed studies will be essential if future generations are to manage salt marshes as ecosystems rather than inventories of plant and animal species. This is especially true in W. Europe where salt marshes may be under the greatest threat from man's activities and where saltmarsh primary production has been virtually ignored as a research topic.

CHAPTER SIX

THE SALTMARSH ECOSYSTEM

It is generally considered that the flow of energy through those herbivores feeding on higher plants on salt marshes is rather small, less than 10% (Smalley, 1960; Teal, 1962; Odum and Heald, 1975). The majority of the plant material dies and is either washed out of the salt marsh or is decomposed *in situ*. Decomposition will be examined in detail before nutrient cycling and energy flow within the saltmarsh ecosystem are discussed.

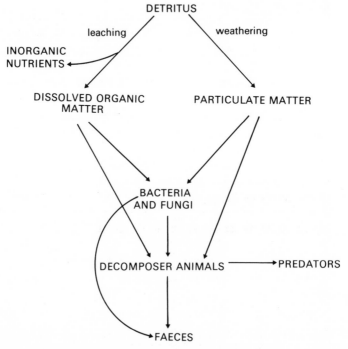

Figure 6.1 Summary of the breakdown process of detritus.

6.1   Decomposition

Dead material is broken down gradually to smaller and smaller particles (Fig. 6.1) and eventually to small molecules. The decomposition process involves the action of abiotic forces, such as weathering and leaching, and the activities of micro-organisms and detritivorous animals. A general introduction to the process is provided by Mason (1977).

Litter within a salt marsh is derived from a number of sources (Perkins, 1974). The most important, in terms of mass, are the higher plants of the marsh. The attached algae, such as *Enteromorpha*, may also be important, while algae growing subtidally may be washed on to the salt marsh. Smaller detrital particles, derived from epiphytic algae, phytoplankton and the faecal pellets of animals are also significant. In addition, a substantial proportion of the litter within salt marshes may be of terrestrial origin, washed down by rivers and deposited by the tide. Unfortunately, synthetic litter, non-biodegradable rubbish thrown overboard from ships or from sewage works or industry, is becoming an increasing eyesore in many salt marshes (see Figs. 6.2, 6.3).

The overall rate of breakdown of litter can be studied by the paired plots technique, in which dead material is collected and weighed at the beginning of the time interval, while living material is removed from a second plot to prevent an increase of dead material in it. After a known time interval, the dead material in the second plot is removed and weighed and the weight difference between the two plots, divided by time, will give the rate of breakdown of litter. Litter can also be enclosed in bags made of nylon or similar material and the loss in weight over time can be followed. Labelling with radio-isotopes can also be used.

In Fig. 6.4, the rates of breakdown of several higher plant species on an

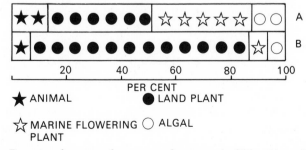

Figure 6.2   Percentage frequency of occurrence of components of litter at two salt marshes in the Solway Firth, north western Britain. (A) Kippford Merse; (B) Glen Isle Merse. Adapted from Perkins (1974).

Figure 6.3 Old wood, paper, tar oil, and glass, plastic or metal containers, not infrequently of toxic chemicals, are among the common garbage dumped into maritime waters. They are subsequently washed on to the salt marshes, sometimes to depths of half a metre, and may completely obliterate the vegetation. Here, flotsam has been washed on to the high water mark of a salt marsh of the River Colne Estuary, E. England.

American east coast salt marsh are compared with that of dead crabs, *Uca pugnax*, using the litter bag technique. The crabs decayed much more rapidly than vegetable material. The soft-tissued *Salicornia* also decayed fairly rapidly, but the breakdown rate of the hard-leaved *Spartina* and *Juncus* was very low. The estimated half-life for decomposition of *Spartina alterniflora* tissue in various marshes on the east coast of the United States is shown in Table 6.1.

The overall rate of breakdown of litter is determined by weight loss, but the constituent parts of the tissue may decompose at different rates. Cruz and Gabriel (1974) examined the decomposition of leaves of the rush *Juncus roemerianus* from a Mississippi salt marsh. The overall breakdown rate, in litter bags, was 40 % per year. Leaf material of different ages (live

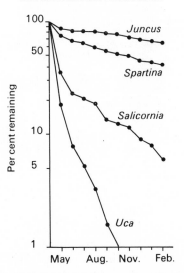

Figure 6.4 Decomposition of dead material of three saltmarsh plants and a crab (*Uca*) in a Georgia, U.S.A., salt marsh (adapted from Odum and de la Cruz, 1967).

young, live mature, standing dead, partially decayed, decomposed coarse and particulate) was analysed for various constituents and the overall changes are shown in Table 6.2. The calorific content of the material increased, which was difficult to explain. It may have been due to the retention of a high organic biomass or to an increase in the microflora on

Table 6.1 The estimated half life for the decomposition of *Spartina alterniflora* tissue in salt marshes in the United States. Linthurst and Reimold (1978*b*) and Reimold *et al.* (1975*a*) used harvested plots to estimate decomposition; the other studies used litter bags.

Location	Position in marsh	Half-life (days)	Reference
Maine	Low	18	Linthurst and Reimold (1978*b*)
	High	51	Linthurst and Reimold (1978*b*)
Georgia	Creek	150	Burkholder and Bornside (1957)
	High	100	Reimold *et al.* (1975*a*)
	Low	35	Reimold *et al.* (1975*a*)
Louisiana	High	130	Kirby and Gosselink (1976)
	Low	70	Kirby and Gosselink (1976)
	Low	45	White *et al.* (1978)
Florida	Low	30	Kruczynski *et al.* (1979)
	Mid	30	Kruczynski *et al.* (1979)
	High	120	Kruczynski *et al.* (1979)
	Creek	25	Kruczynski *et al.* (1979)

Table 6.2 The changes in content (%) of constituents of *Juncus* leaf material of various ages (young to particulate detritus) collected from a Mississippi salt marsh (from data in Cruz and Gabriel, 1974).

	Initial %	Final %
Carbon	49.75	6.38
Phosphorus	0.22	0.17
Carbohydrate	52.0	11.0
Fats	2.0	0.9
Nitrogen	1.09	0.57
Crude fibre	37.0	9.0
Protein	9.0	4.0

the detritus. All other constituents declined. Different carbohydrates may decompose at different rates. For example, breakdown of the cellulose fraction of *Spartina alterniflora* litter was three times faster than the lignin fraction, with 32.1% and 10.6% respectively mineralized after 720 h of incubation (Maccubbin and Hodson, 1980).

Cruz and Gabriel (1974) placed the particulate detritus of *Juncus roemerianus* into incubation bottles at 30°C. Some 50% of this material decomposed in 36 days and there were significant decreases in organic content and carbon. However, the nitrogen content of detritus increased, due to the conversion of plant tissue to microbial protein, as the bacterial population increased on the detritus particles; such an increase in nitrogen during decomposition has been widely reported. Adsorption of materials on to the surface of the litter may also occur. Pellenbarg (1978) and Breteler *et al.* (1981) have reported enrichments of mercury, zinc, copper and iron on *Spartina alterniflora* litter. These overall changes in the constituents of litter make it a very different source of food for animals compared to the growing plant.

In the early stages of decomposition, the dead material loses weight very quickly (see Fig. 6.4). This is due to the leaching out of minerals and dissolved organic matter (DOM) in the first few weeks after death. Leaching of organic matter also occurs from living plants and Gallagher *et al.* (1976) estimate that 61 kg ha^{-1} y^{-1} is leached by the tide from *Spartina alterniflora* stands. DOM is attacked very rapidly by bacteria, though some materials are more resistant than others. The remaining particulate organic matter (POM) is subject to weathering, a physical breakdown caused by tides, winds and temperature and helped by structural weakening caused by chemical action and by the activities of animals. The resultant smaller particles are much more amenable to attack by micro-organisms as they have a larger surface area relative to mass.

The bacteria are the most important organisms in terms of the quantity of mineralization they carry out and they are essential for driving the element cycles within the salt marsh. Fungi appear to be less important in marine habitats than in terrestrial habitats, though phycomycetes are widespread and their functional role may have been underestimated.

The efficiency of conversion of *Spartina alterniflora* to microbial biomass has been studied in the laboratory by Gosselink and Kirby (1974). They collected dead, standing stems and leaves of *Spartina*, dried them and divided them with sieves into four particle size fractions, with mean diameters of 67 μm, 111 μm, 163 μm and 213 μm. These fractions were incubated in inoculated sea water at 30°C in the dark. Over a 30-day period, the particulate nitrogen, oxidizable carbon, dry weight and metabolic rate were determined. The biomass of *Spartina* and microbes was calculated by solving simultaneous equations which described the distribution of particulate nitrogen and mass in each culture. Assuming that the particulate contents of a flask were a mixture of microbial cells and dead *Spartina*, the distribution of mass in the culture could be described by the equation:

$$C_d = C_s + C_m \qquad (6.1)$$

where C_d is the ash-free dry weight (AFDW)/volume of
     particulate material
    C_s is the AFDW/volume of *Spartina*
    C_m is the AFDW/volume of micro-organisms.

The particulate nitrogen distribution in the culture can be described by:

$$N_d \times C_d = (N_m + C_m) \times (N_s \times C_s) \qquad (6.2)$$

where N is the nitrogen fraction and the subscripts are as above. Analyses were carried out at different times during the incubation to determine C_d and N_d. The nitrogen content at the start of the experiment was taken as N_s and was assumed to remain constant. N_m, the average nitrogen content in the micro-organisms, was taken as 13%, the upper range of a number of values recorded in the literature, and was also assumed to remain constant. The equations were solved for the concentration of *Spartina* (C_s) and micro-organisms (C_m).

Gosselink and Kirby observed a decrease in *Spartina* tissue and a build-up in micro-organisms (Fig. 6.5). The smaller particles, with their greater surface area to mass ratio, supported a more rapid microbial growth than

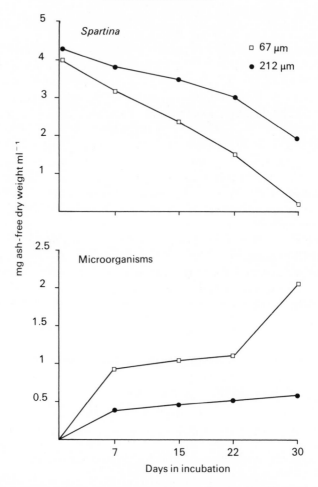

Figure 6.5 Decrease of *Spartina* substrate and increase in microbial biomass in incubated detritus of two initial particle sizes (adapted from Gosselink and Kirby, 1974).

the larger particles and they degraded more rapidly. The efficiency of conversion of *Spartina* to microbial biomass ranged from 28 % in the larger particles to 60 % in the smaller particles over the 30 days of the experiment and the low-protein *Spartina* detritus was converted to a high-protein microbial biomass.

Detritus is a relatively poor source of food for micro-organisms, so that they must augment the essential nutrients they obtain from their substrate by assimilating dissolved minerals in the surrounding medium. The detritus is thereby enriched in terms of a food source for animals. Detritus particles are not, as once thought, coated with bacteria. Fenchel and Harrison (1976) have reported that only 2–15 % of the detrital surface is covered by bacteria, corresponding to 10^9 to 10^{10} bacteria per gram dry weight of detritus, depending on particle size.

Fresh detritus is invaded rapidly by the microfauna. Flagellate protozoans reach a peak within 200 hours of inoculation, followed closely by ciliates (Fenchel and Harrison, 1976). These small animals feed largely on bacteria, ungrazed cultures having greater bacterial densities than grazed systems (Harrison and Mann, 1975). Nevertheless, grazing stimulates the rate of decomposition of detritus. Barley hay had almost completely disappeared after 1000 h in the presence of a natural assemblage of protozoans, whereas a pure bacterial culture decomposed only 20 % of the hay over the same period of time (Fenchel and Harrison, 1976). Hunt et al. (1977) suggest that the grazing of bacteria by protozoans is analogous to growing bacteria in continuous culture. A continuous, optimal production of bacteria is achieved by removing them at a rate which balances their rate of growth, such that the period of exponential growth of bacteria is extended.

The larger consumers take in detritus, together with bacteria, fungi, epiphytic diatoms and the microfauna, a much richer food source than the detritus alone. Much recent evidence suggests that it is the epiphytic assemblage which forms the prime nutritional source for detritivores. Fenchel (1970) found that the amphipod *Parhyalella whelpleyi* ate detrital particles of turtle grass *Thalassia testudinum*, but assimilated only microbial material, passing the plant material out undigested. *Gammarus oceanicus* would not feed on *Zostera marina* leaves which had been stripped of epibionts, though it readily grazed untreated leaves (Harrison, 1977). *Orchestia grillus* and *Mucrogammarus* sp., again amphipods, also appear to feed only on the microbial component of litter (Lopez et al., 1977; Morrison and White, 1980), while Kofoed (1975) made similar observations on the prosobranch snail *Hydrobia ventrosa*. Feeding solely on micro-organisms may not be a universal feature of marine detritivores, however. The shrimp *Palaemonetes pugio* assimilates both detritus and microbes (Adams and Angelovic, 1970), while a re-inoculation of the faeces with bacteria occurs in the hind-gut (Johannes and Satomi, 1966). Tenore (1981) suggests that the polychaete *Capitella capitata* can utilize the detritus from seaweeds directly, because it is rich in available nitrogen, but that detritus from higher plants requires protein enrichment by micro-organisms. Clearly, a greater range of detritivores will need to be examined before the importance of detritus as a direct food source can be assessed.

If detritivorous animals do not obtain their requirements directly from dead higher plant material, but indirectly via micro-organisms, then we need to determine whether they accelerate or retard the decomposition process. The weight of evidence suggests, as with the microfauna, that grazing of micro-organisms stimulates the rate of breakdown of detritus. Many detritivores comminute the detritus on which they feed, producing a substrate with a larger surface area, allowing more micro-organisms to colonize. Fenchel (1970) showed that this mechanical activity doubled the oxygen consumption in cultures in four days when *Parhyalella whelpleyi* fed on *Thalassia testudinum* detritus. However, animals do not necessarily stimulate microbial growth merely by providing a greater surface area. Morrison and White (1980) found that the amphipod *Mucrogammarus* did not alter the surface area of detritus by comminution, but increased the biomass and activity of micro-organisms, suggesting that grazing maintained them in a state of physiological youth. *Mucrogammarus* also altered the structure of the microbial community. Although selective feeding did not occur, the slower-growing fungi were reduced in numbers, to be replaced by the faster-growing bacteria.

The material not digested by animals will be voided as faeces, initially having a low microbial population. The faeces will quickly become colonized by bacteria, and Hargrave (1976) has shown that faecal respiration is markedly higher than that of the substrate on which the animals fed,

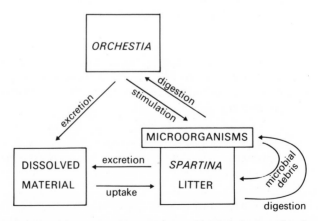

Figure 6.6 Postulated interactions between the amphipod *Orchestia grillus*, *Spartina* litter and micro-organisms (after Lopez *et al.*, 1977).

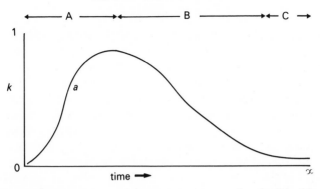

Figure 6.7 Generalized sequence of decay rates (see text for details). Adapted from Godshalk and Wetzel (1978).

though it returned to substrate level after several days. The reworking, by deposit feeders, of detritus and sediment thus provides space for microbial growth and enhances the food supply of the animals. The burrowing activities of animals extend the depth of the aerobic zone in sediments.

Invertebrates excrete large amounts of nitrogen and phosphorus, which are in short supply to micro-organisms living on detritus. These dissolved nutrients can be taken up immediately by bacteria, thus stimulating growth. Lopez *et al.* (1977) have produced a simple model showing the interactions between the amphipod *Orchestia grillus*, micro-organisms and *Spartina* litter (Fig. 6.6) which emphasizes the feedback loops and internal buffering mechanisms within the system. For example, *Orchestia* both stimulate and digest micro-organisms, while they excrete dissolved materials which are taken up by the microbes.

Godshalk and Wetzel (1978), from a study of the breakdown of *Zostera marina* and other aquatic macrophytes, have developed a generalized model of decomposition, in which they recognized three phases in the process (Fig. 6.7). The controlling factors were described in an approximate mathematical form:

$$k = \frac{T \times O \times N}{R \times S}$$

where k = relative decay rate
   T = temperature (°C)
   O = dissolved oxygen
   N = mineral nutrients for microbial growth
   R = initial tissue refractility
   S = particle size (volume/surface area).

In Fig. 6.7, k is defined as the amount of detrital carbon metabolized per unit time, plotted over undefined units of time. Phase A represents a period of increasing weight loss, due to leaching and the release of dissolved organic matter (DOM), as cells lyse. Much of the DOM is labile and rapidly metabolized, the rate of decomposition being influenced by temperature and oxygen. The peak rate of weight loss occurs during phase A. The rate of decomposition decreases to phase B, where weight loss is due to microbial colonization and metabolism. The factors which influence decomposition exert their maximum effect at this time and, as the easily decomposed materials are utilized first, the particulate matter becomes increasingly resistant to decay, while nutrients and dissolved oxygen may also be reduced. In phase C, the breakdown of the remaining resistant material approaches zero and it may be permanently incorporated into the sediments.

The foregoing discussion has shown how complex are the interrelations between the decomposer organisms, their substrate, and one another. Reviews have been provided by Christian and Wetzel (1981) and Lee (1980).

6.2 Saltmarsh sediments and nutrient cycling

The superficial layers of the sediment are generally aerobic and the surface detritus is suspended and stirred by the action of tides. The upper sediments are also re-worked and turned over by the activities of animals. Below a few centimetres, however, the sediment is generally anoxic. The roots of plants oxidize the sediments through the passive release of oxygen. In a *Spartina alterniflora* marsh, the redox potential of sediment in the root zone of the grass was greater than in unvegetated parts or below the root zones, while the sediments underlying the tall form of *Spartina* were more oxidized than those beneath the short form (Howes *et al.*, 1981). A positive feedback appears to be in operation, where areas of sediment that are more oxidized allow higher production by *Spartina*, which then results in increased oxidation in the sediment. The process is probably limited eventually by nutrient availability.

Mechalas (1974) considers that mixed populations of bacteria use oxygen, nitrate, sulphate and carbon dioxide in a decreasing order of preference as electron acceptors and this utilization is related to depth as the availability of successive acceptors becomes depleted. In the aerobic surface sediments, or on the detritus suspended by the tide, oxygen is the electron acceptor and oxygen depletion is replaced by diffusion from the air or water, assisted by the turbulence created by the advancing tide.

Denitrification, respiration using nitrate as an electron acceptor, occurs below the aerobic zone, or in anaerobic microniches within the aerobic zone (Fenchel and Blackburn, 1979). The ammonia generated in anoxic regions may be nitrified when the sediment is exposed to the air, whereas when the sediment is flooded by the tide, oxygen depletion may lead to denitrification. Denitrification proceeds exclusively under anaerobic conditions, while nitrification is an exclusively aerobic process.

Nitrate is used preferentially to sulphate as an electron acceptor, because it yields more energy. As with nitrate reduction, sulphate reduction occurs substantially in oxygen-rich sediments where anaerobic microniches exist, for example in the centre of detritus particles. In anoxic saltmarsh sediments, sulphate is an important electron acceptor. The carbon source is oxidized to carbon dioxide, with hydrogen sulphide release, but complete mineralization may not always occur, with acetate being the end point of metabolism. Recent work has shown that acetate is oxidized to carbon dioxide by sulphate-reducing bacteria in saltmarsh sediments (Widdel and Pfennig, 1977; Banat *et al.*, 1981). The reduction of sulphate produces sulphide, which is stable in anaerobic conditions, where it may react with iron to precipitate ferrous sulphide. After diagenesis*, pyrite (FeS_2), a stable mineral not subject to auto-oxidation, is formed. However, only a small proportion of sulphide is usually precipitated, there being a diffusion of sulphide to the aerobic sediment, where it may auto-oxidize or be biologically oxidized, forming an electron donor for some bacteria. In an Essex salt marsh, sulphate reduction in the top 20 cm of sediment in a creek bottom amounted to 144 g sulphate-S $m^{-2} y^{-1}$, while in a saltmarsh pan it was 99 g sulphate-S $m^{-2} y^{-1}$ (Nedwell and Abram, 1978). In sediment in Limfjord, Denmark, sulphate-respiring bacteria accounted for approximately 23 % of carbon oxidation, compared with 75 % for the more efficient oxygen-respiring bacteria. The remaining 2 % of carbon oxidation was due to nitrate-respiring bacteria (Fenchel and Blackburn, 1979).

Carbon dioxide serves as the terminal electron acceptor for the anaerobic oxidation of molecular hydrogen, or organic compounds such as acetate, to methane, the process of methanogenesis. Methane production occurs only at depths where sulphate reduction is limited by a supply of available sulphates and it appears that methanogenic bacteria are inhibited by sulphate-reducing bacteria due to competition for the limited

---

* The processes (physical, chemical or biological) that bring about changes in a sediment subsequent to deposition in water (Berner, 1980).

amount of hydrogen produced in saltmarsh sediments (Abram and Nedwell, 1978a, b). Methanogenesis is small compared with sulphate reduction in salt marshes, amounting to 1 g CH-C $m^{-2} y^{-1}$ (Atkinson and Hall, 1976). Sulphate reduction is therefore the major terminal oxidation step in the sulphate-rich sediments of salt marshes, compared to freshwater sediments, where methanogenesis is very important.

In summary, the dissimilation of organic carbon is carried out aerobically, in the topmost sediments of the salt marsh and in the overlying water in pans or at high tide, and anaerobically in deeper sediments or in anoxic micro-niches in top sediments. There are few estimates of turnover time for carbon. In a *Spartina alterniflora* marsh in North Carolina, Cammen (1976) estimated a turnover time of organic carbon of between 3.7 and 4.5 years, though the accumulated material originated from a number of sources additional to *Spartina*. The decomposition process results in the release of nutrients which may then be recycled within the ecosystem. Nitrogen and phosphorus are normally limiting to plant growth, so that the cycling of these elements will be described as examples of the process.

Nitrogen is the limiting nutrient in many salt marshes (Valiela and Teal, 1974) and additions of nitrogen stimulate primary production, decomposition and the growth rate of animals feeding within the salt marsh. In an aerobic sediment in a Danish salt marsh dominated by *Halimione portulacoides*, Henriksen and Jensen (1979) found that the nitrate made available for plant growth was generated almost entirely within the sediments, with little tidal import. There appeared to be a net export of ammonia. Very little of the nitrate accumulated during nitrification was used in the internal bacterial nitrogen cycle, because of the preference of bacteria for ammonia, so that the nitrate was available for plants. From laboratory studies of intact sediment cores, the net mineralization of nitrogen was estimated at 11 g N $m^{-2} y^{-1}$, of which 80% was converted to nitrate during the growing season.

Most saltmarsh sediments are predominantly anaerobic and little nitrification occurs, ammonium presumably forming the chief source of nitrogen for plants. However, the role of the oxidized microzone around plant roots in microbial nitrogen conversions has not been investigated and substantial nitrate could be generated here. In an Essex salt marsh, with a mixed plant community, Abd. Aziz and Nedwell (1979) found evidence of little nitrogen fixation or nitrification in the predominantly anaerobic sediment and concluded that the majority of nitrogen was cycled within the salt marsh between organic nitrogen and ammonium fractions. Valiela and Teal (1979) have provided a detailed nitrogen budget for a salt marsh, dominated by *Spartina alterniflora*, in Massachusetts. They recorded substantial imports of nitrate in ground and rain water, while there was a smaller addition of nitrogen due to nitrogen fixation. Nitrogen was also brought on to the marsh on the flood tide. Denitrification and the ebb-tide removed substantial amounts of nitrogen. The import of nitrogen amounted to $1482\,\mathrm{kg\,ha^{-1}\,y^{-1}}$, and the output to $1530\,\mathrm{kg\,ha^{-1}\,y^{-1}}$, resulting in a net annual export of $28\,\mathrm{kg\,ha^{-1}\,y^{-1}}$. Woodwell *et al.* (1979) similarly recorded a net export, of $9\,\mathrm{kg\,ha^{-1}\,y^{-1}}$ inorganic nitrogen only, for a *Spartina* salt marsh in New York. In the Massachusetts marsh, nitrogen flowed from the ground water to the sea during the winter, but during the spring little nitrate escaped from the marsh. Ammonia was lost during the summer, probably by the leaching of soluble nitrogen from *Spartina*. Losses of nitrogen in autumn derived from the decay of senescent material.

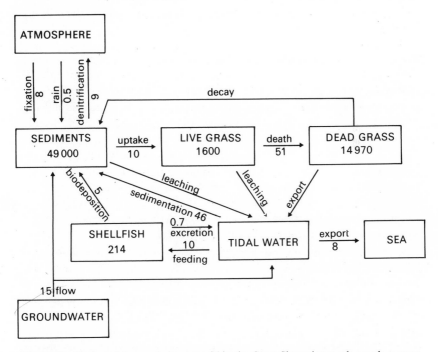

Figure 6.8   Pools and fluxes of nitrogen within the Great Sippewissett salt marsh, eastern U.S.A. Quantities are in kgN for the whole marsh ($226\,000\,\mathrm{m^2}$), fluxes are kg day^{-1}, for one day in early August (adapted from Valiela and Teal, 1979).

To quantify the interconversions within the salt marsh, Valiela and Teal considered the data for a typical August day (Fig. 6.8). At this time of year, the marsh intercepted more nitrogen than it released. The sediment represented the largest nitrogen pool, while the underground parts of plants contained twice as much nitrogen as the above-ground parts. The nitrogen loss from the vegetation through leaching was equivalent to the uptake. There was a large amount of detritus, from the previous year's growth, remaining on the marsh. Much of this was suspended on the incoming tide and it could be sedimented within the marsh or consumed by bivalves. This suspended matter was equivalent to $0.44\,kg\,N\,ha^{-1}\,day^{-1}$. The bivalves deposited particles, as faeces, on the marsh and these were not readily suspended, but they excreted ammonia to the sea, equivalent to 25 % of the nitrogen loss from the marsh.

Nitrogen cycling within salt marshes is still poorly understood. Differences in the relative importance of the individual processes, such as nitrification and denitrification, are undoubtedly dependent on local conditions and it would be unwise to make generalizations about the nitrogen budgets of salt marshes.

A generalized diagram of the phosphorus cycle in a salt marsh is shown in Fig. 6.9. It is much simpler than the nitrogen cycle, phosphorus being taken up and used by organisms as phosphate, and also liberated as phosphate by excretion or the decomposition of dead matter. Phosphorus is frequently limiting to plant growth, so plants have developed efficient mechanisms of uptake. The turnover time of phosphate can be very short, a matter of a few minutes when biological activity is high. However, phosphorus forms insoluble compounds and organic phosphate esters, which are very resistant to hydrolysis, so limiting the available phosphorus to the ecosystem. Bacteria play an essential role in phosphorus availability by indirectly mediating the release of dissolved orthophosphate from insoluble phosphates (Fenchel and Blackburn, 1979).

Reimold (1972) labelled sediments in a Georgia salt marsh with ^{32}P and studied its uptake and dissipation through Spartina alterniflora. The uptake of phosphorus was greatest in the deeper parts of the sediment, around 100 cm, where most of the roots and rhizomes were situated. The plants released phosphorus into incoming tidal water, the maximum rate of loss occurring 10–15 days after the introduction of the isotope, with very little remaining after a month. Reimold considered that Spartina was acting as a nutrient pump, absorbing phosphorus from the sediments and releasing it to the estuarine water with the tide. This could amount to a maximum transfer of $6\,kg\,P\,ha^{-1}\,day^{-1}$ during the peak growing season

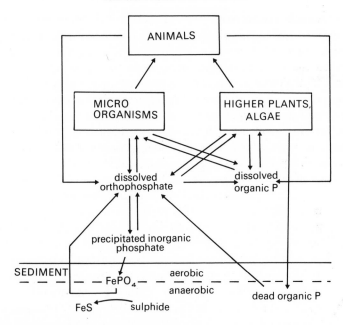

Figure 6.9 Phosphorus cycle in a salt marsh.

for *Spartina*, though it was much less when there was incomplete tidal cover, or during the winter.

It has already been mentioned that bivalves deposit substantial amounts of nitrogen on to salt marshes. The role of the mussel *Modiolus demissus* in phosphorus cycling has been studied by Kuenzler (1961a). Mussels feed by filtering suspended matter out of the water at high tide. The material is graded by the cilia and rejected particles are passed out as pseudofaeces, which together with the faeces are bound in mucus and deposited on the marsh surface. *Modiolus* was relatively insignificant in energy flow in the salt marsh, accounting for some 0.8 % of the total. However, one-third of the particulate phosphorus was removed from suspension in the water and deposited on the marsh surface, where it was made available to other organisms.

Woodwell and Whitney (1977) and Woodwell *et al.* (1979) have provided a phosphorus budget for a salt marsh in New York. Over the year, the budget was approximately in balance, but there was a marked seasonality in the movement of inorganic phosphorus, with an influx during the winter and a loss during the summer. There was an overall influx of organic phosphorus. The net loss of phosphorus approximated $28\,kg\,ha^{-1}\,y^{-1}$, though a substantial statistical error surrounds this value.

6.3 Energy flow

The limit to the amount of energy contained within an ecosystem is the efficiency of the photosynthetic process. The photosynthetic efficiency (the ratio of carbon dioxide assimilated to quanta of photosynthetically active radiation) of two saltmarsh communities, dominated by C_4 grasses, in Maryland averaged 1.9% (Drake and Read, 1981).

There are two basic approaches to the study of energy flow through an ecosystem. The first is to study one or two species in detail; they are usually chosen as key species which are thought to be promoters of energy flow through the system. After a series of such studies it may be possible to construct an energy budget for the system as a whole. The alternative approach is to study all components of an ecosystem together at a less detailed level, making use of short-cut methods. There are rarely sufficient resources available to carry out an in depth study at one time over an entire ecosystem, which is the ideal approach to energy flow studies.

One of the earliest attempts at constructing an energy budget of key species in a salt marsh was that of Odum and Smalley (1959), comparing a herbivorous grasshopper, *Orchelimum fidicinium*, with a detritus-feeding snail, *Littorina irrorata*. The production of the grasshopper population was estimated at $117\,kJ\,m^{-2}\,y^{-1}$ and 1% of the net production of *Spartina* was assimilated by this species. The production of the snail population was estimated at $1212\,kJ\,m^{-2}\,y^{-1}$, suggesting that most energy is dissipated through detritivores rather than through herbivores in a salt marsh. These energy flow figures were obtained for the favourable areas of the marsh, not for the marsh as a whole.

In the same Georgia salt marsh, Kuenzler (1961*b*) estimated the net production of the mussel *Modiolus demissus* at $70\,kJ\,m^{-2}\,y^{-1}$, while annual respiration amounted to $163\,kJ\,m^{-2}\,y^{-1}$, 70% of the assimilated energy of $234\,kJ\,m^{-2}\,y^{-1}$. It was described above how the mussel is of greater significance in nutrient cycling than in promoting energy flow.

In a North Carolina salt marsh, the key animal species were considered to be the fiddler crabs *Uca pugnax* and *U. minax* and the snail *Littorina irrorata* (Cammen *et al.*, 1980). Together, the three species consumed approximately one-third of the net primary production and assimilated about one-tenth of this amount, about 3.4% of the net production. Much of the material ingested by these deposit feeders may be reingested several times, so that comparatively little of the net production passes directly through them. Cammen *et al.* (1980) stressed that the chief role of these animals is in reworking the sediments and promoting nutrient cycling and decomposition.

Welsh (1975) studied the ecology of the shrimp *Palaemonetes pugio*, found in an embayment within a salt marsh in New England. Energy flow through the shrimp population was estimated at $1983 \, \text{kJ} \, \text{m}^{-2} \, \text{y}^{-1}$. Ice, during February and March, pushed large amounts of dead *Spartina* from the salt marsh into the embayment. The shrimps ingested these periodic surpluses and prevented excessive accumulations of material. However, the *Spartina* released annually into the embayment satisfied only one-third of the energy demands of the shrimps, which also fed extensively on algae and the aquatic macrophyte *Ruppia*. The shrimps ingested, on average, $12.1 \, \text{kJ} \, \text{m}^{-2}$ of food, of which $3.3 \, \text{kJ} \, \text{m}^{-2}$ was deposited as faeces and $2.9 \, \text{kJ} \, \text{m}^{-2}$ released as dissolved organic matter, only $0.8 \, \text{kJ} \, \text{m}^{-2}$ contributing to production. Thus, much of the food ingested by the shrimps quickly became available as an ideal substrate for the growth of bacteria and diatoms.

A summary of the energy flow through some animals living in salt marshes is given in Table 6.3.

The first attempt to study energy flow through an entire ecosystem was that of Teal (1962), on the Georgia salt marsh mentioned above. Only 1.4% of the incident light energy was converted to net production by *Spartina alterniflora*, amounting to $27\,500 \, \text{kJ} \, \text{m}^{-2} \, \text{y}^{-1}$, while an additional $6770 \, \text{kJ} \, \text{m}^{-2} \, \text{y}^{-1}$ net productivity was due to algae. Herbivores consumed only $1275 \, \text{kJ} \, \text{m}^{-2} \, \text{y}^{-1}$ *Spartina* (4.6%), the remainder entering the detritus pathway. Some 55% of net primary productivity was dissipated by consumers, 47% being due to bacteria. The remaining detritus ($15\,422 \, \text{kJ} \, \text{m}^{-2} \, \text{y}^{-1}$) was considered as export.

Teal's study concentrated on energy flow in the high salt marsh, whereas a study by Nixon and Oviatt (1973) detailed the occurrences in the creeks and embayments which link salt marshes to coastal waters. In this New England salt marsh, great differences occurred between summer and winter. The detrital pathway was the most important for the dissipation of energy. Primary production by algae and macrophytes occurred seasonally, but over the year the embayment community was a net consumer of material imported from the emergent marsh. One of the main consumers was the shrimp *Palaemonetes pugio*, described above. The energy budget for the embayment is summarized in Table 6.4. The excess consumption in the embayment amounted to 14% of the total production

Table 6.3 A summary of the energy flow through some salt marsh animals (kJ m^{-2} y^{-1}).

Species	Locality	Production	Respiration	Total energy	Source
Orchelimum fidicinium	Georgia	46	79	125	Smalley (1960)
Littorina irrorata	Georgia	121	1091	1212	Odum and Smalley (1959)
Littorina irrorata	North Carolina	33	389	422	Cammen et al (1980)
L. irrorata, Melampus bidentatus, Neritina reclivata	Louisiana	167	982	1149	Day et al. (1973)
Littorina saxatilis	Nova Scotia	25	—	—	Burke and Mann (1974)
Melampus lineatus	Nova Scotia	18	—	—	Burke and Mann (1974)
Mytilus edulis	Nova Scotia	59	—	—	Burke and Mann (1974)
Modiolus demissus	Georgia	71	163	234	Kuenzler (1961b)
Uca pugnax	North Carolina	213	230	453	Cammen et al. (1980)
U. minax	North Carolina	54	184	238	Cammen et al. (1980)
U. pugnax, U. pugilator, Sesarma reticulatum	Georgia	146	715	861	Teal (1962)
U. pugnax, S. reticulatum, Callinectes sapidus	Louisiana	54	456	510	Day et al. (1973)
Palaemonetes pugio	New England	305	1678	1983	Welsh (1975)

Table 6.4 Annual energy budget $(kJ\,m^{-2}\,y^{-1} \times 10^3)$ for the Bissel Cove marsh embayment, New England (adapted from Nixon and Oviatt, 1973).

Production of organic matter within embayment	40.2
Consumption of organic matter within embayment	41.0
Excess of consumption over production	0.8
Imports from: emergent marsh	1.0
streams	0.062
immigration of fish and shrimps	0.014
Total import	1.08
Excess organic matter available for storage and export	0.25

of the emergent marsh; some 10–30 % of production was potentially available for export to the estuary.

Howarth and Teal (1980) have pointed out that, in partially anoxic ecosystems such as salt marshes, energy flow cannot be described entirely in terms of the movement of organic carbon, because the reduced inorganic end products of anaerobic respiration contain significant quantities of energy. In New England salt marshes, reduced inorganic sulphur compounds are important in energy flow. Howarth and Teal consider that the export of energy from peat as reduced inorganic sulphur compounds may be twice the net above-ground production by *Spartina alterniflora*.

6.4 Export

The early studies of energy flow through salt marshes have considered that there is a net export of particulate organic carbon to estuaries and coastal waters (Schelski and Odum, 1961; Teal, 1962; Odum and de la Cruz, 1967). The exported material fuels the food web, that leading to fish and hence to man being considered especially important. This export to estuaries has been one of the prime arguments in favour of conserving salt marshes and protecting them from reclamation and development. Some recent work has contradicted this concept and has been unable to demonstrate a net export of particulate carbon (Heinle and Flemer, 1976; Woodwell *et al.*, 1977; Settlemyre and Gardner, 1977; Haines, 1977, 1979), though other work has demonstrated a net export (Day *et al.*, 1973; Nixon and Oviatt, 1973; Valiela *et al.*, 1978a). Daly and Mathieson (1981) report a net import of organic matter on to a salt marsh. A review is provided by Nixon (1980).

Other materials may behave differently from organic carbon. A net export of nitrogen has been described by Heinle and Flemer (1976),

Woodwell *et al.* (1977, 1979), Valiela and Teal (1979) and Henriksen and Jensen (1979), while Trattner and Mattson (1976) and Daly and Mathieson (1981) reported significant imports. Net exports of phosphorus were recorded by Reimold (1972) and Heinle and Flemer (1976), while a net balance was reported by Woodwell and Whitney (1977) and Daly and Mathieson (1981). There are diurnal, tidal and seasonal influences on the direction of flow of materials in a salt marsh and some of these have been described earlier. The measurement of movement of materials is therefore extremely difficult. Gallagher *et al.* (1980) emphasize that the export characteristics of a salt marsh will depend on the community type, the physiography of the marsh and on the element under consideration.

Haines (1977, 1979) has been one of the main challengers of the concept of salt marshes as net exporters. A study of carbon ratios ($^{12}C/^{13}C$, see Chapter 4) of the suspended material in an estuary pointed to the majority of material being derived from algal production. Haines considered that algal production within estuaries had been underestimated. In Georgia estuaries, the combined input of organic matter from phytoplankton ($770 \, g \, m^{-2} \, y^{-1}$) and detritus from terrestrial plants ($600 \, g \, m^{-2} \, y^{-1}$) was comparable to the supposed detrital input ($780–1660 \, g \, m^{-2} \, y^{-1}$) from *Spartina* marshes. Haines (1979) concluded that salt marshes have a minor role in promoting secondary production within estuaries. She suggested, however, at high tide, many fishes move on to salt marshes to feed and avoid predators, so that the export of organic carbon may be significant, but in the form of living animals rather than as organic detritus.

A number of factors, however, may be operating to determine whether salt marshes are net exporters or importers of materials (Odum *et al.*, 1979). The geomorphology of the drainage basin and the relative magnitudes of tidal range and freshwater throughput are of particular importance. Marshes surrounding basins with only a narrow channel to the open sea, and little freshwater throughput, are likely to be net importers. V-shaped estuaries, widening and deepening towards the mouth, with a large throughput of fresh water, are likely to be net exporters. There are many drainage basins between these two extremes (see Chapter 1). Odum *et al.* (1979) also point out that storms are particularly important in determining export, large amounts of matter being removed by a combination of elevated tides, wind and heavy rainfall, these conditions rarely being monitored by scientists. It is clearly very unwise to generalize about the role of salt marshes as either sources or sinks of materials to neighbouring coastal waters.

CHAPTER SEVEN

CONSERVATION OF SALT MARSHES

Natural salt marsh remains one of the least modified of habitats in developed countries such as Britain. Salt marshes have a great aesthetic interest despite their prevailing flatness. The vast pink expanses of *Armeria maritima* in early summer followed in late summer by the purple of *Limonium* spp. are remarked upon by many coastal visitors with no particular interest in conservation. The desolate beauty of these coastlands has already been alluded to in Chapter 1.

Salt marshes have relatively simple plant communities, making them ideal places for teaching the principles of ecology and for research. Such research is not entirely esoteric. For example, saltmarsh plants live in a habitat tolerated by few species and a knowledge of their adaptations to high salinity may help us solve some of the problems of growing crops under irrigation in arid countries, where vast areas of land become uncultivable due to increases in soil salinity. Indeed, these plants represent a genetic resource which may be utilized in crop improvement by future generations, using gene technology.

Salt marshes are highly productive ecosystems. Wetlands as a whole produce 2.3 % of the world's net productivity, though they occupy only 0.4 % of the world's area (Lieth and Whittaker, 1975). Only tropical rain-forests equal the net productivity of salt marshes, when measured in terms of $g m^{-2} y^{-1}$. In the north temperate region, salt marshes form a substantial proportion of the total wetland habitat. On the east coast of the United States, for example, 85 % of all wetlands are salt marshes (Reimold, 1977; Marinucci, 1982).

We have seen that salt marshes interact intimately with the coastal waters on which they abut. In many estuaries there is a net outflow of materials to intertidal flats and coastal waters, sustaining a dense inverte-brate fauna to feed wading birds and fish, especially the larval stages. The invertebrates include commercially important species, such as the cockle (*Cerastoderme edule*) and oyster (*Ostrea edulis*). Few of the wading birds feed within the salt marsh, preferring the open flats, but at high tide salt marshes provide a safe refuge for the roosting flocks, being of difficult and often dangerous access to man, due to the intersecting creeks brimming with muddy and swiftly flowing water. Safe roosting sites are at a premium in many estuaries (Prater, 1981), due to disturbance.

In addition to fuelling inshore fisheries, salt marshes are of value to local communities, providing pasture for livestock, turf, hay for winter fodder, or the cultivation of shellfish within creeks (Queen, 1977). These traditional uses are compatible with, or may even improve, the conservation value of salt marshes. Salt marshes are also important in coastal defences, friction dissipating much of the energy of the tide as water flows over the vegetation (p. 18). At 1981 prices, the building of a sea wall, fronted by salt marsh, cost some £14 000 per km. A wall not protected by salt marsh needs much more reinforcement and could cost up to £300 000 per km, some 20 times more (unpublished data, Anglian Water Authority).

It is almost impossible to put a financial value to salt marshes, though the value to a developer is more easily determined. Gosselink et al. (1974) estimated an approximate quantitative dollar return, for the east coast salt marshes of the United States, of $10 250 ha^{-1} y^{-1}, whereas $247 000 ha^{-1} was paid for a salt marsh in New Jersey to develop a sports complex. Meyers and Dolphin (1977) estimated the damage to fisheries and recreation at 12–19 million dollars if the salt marshes of the Fraser River estuary, British Columbia, were reclaimed.

Because of the difficulty of assigning financial values to the retention of salt marshes compared to the comparative ease of valuing their development, there are major threats to salt marshes in the forms of reclamation, development and pollution.

7.1 Reclamation for agriculture

The reclamation of intertidal lands for agriculture has been carried out for centuries. In Essex, eastern England, more than 15 000 ha of salt marsh have been reclaimed (Nature Conservancy Council, unpublished), while in the Wash 470 km^2 of land have been reclaimed since Saxon times, an area larger than the 314 km^2 of salt marsh and intertidal flats which remain (Natural Environment Research Council, 1976). Over the last 30 years, 15 % of the salt marsh in England and Wales has been lost and there is a potential threat to a further 20 %. Similarly, in the United States, 800 000 ha of salt marsh, approximately 25 % of the total, was destroyed between 1932 and 1954 (Teal and Teal, 1969).

Reclamation is usually achieved by enclosing high marsh within a sea

Figure 7.1 Reclaimed salt marsh, Colne estuary, Essex. High marsh has been enclosed within the sea wall and the field has been under drained to provide ideal growing conditions for winter cereals.

wall (Fig. 7.1), although more recent trends have involved reclaiming intertidal flats as well. Once the salt has leached away the land can be planted with crops and, since the sediment is alluvial, it is very fertile. Deposition of silt frequently takes place on the seaward edge of the sea wall, with a new salt marsh extending into the mudflats, so that the salt marsh area may remain relatively constant. However it is frequently maintained in an immature state, as in the Wash (Natural Environment Research Council, 1976).

Most agricultural reclamation in Europe is grant-aided by government, ostensibly in the interests of greater food production to benefit society as a whole. However, the crops usually grown on these fertile sites are in surplus so that benefits accrue to the individual landowner alone, while society pays a guaranteed price for food it does not need and then pays for the storage of that surplus in intervention. Large areas of reclaimed land, for instance in the Wash, are put down to bulb production, which further belies the claims of government (H.M.S.O. 1975, 1979) that reclamation is essential for increasing food production. The cost of reclamation is that many sites of *international* importance for conservation, part of our national heritage, are lost forever. About 4000 ha of salt marsh in Britain, classified as Sites of Special Scientific Interest, have been reclaimed since 1950.

In England, for example, two internationally important salt marshes have recently been saved from reclamation, but at a price. Some 2200 ha of salt marsh and mudflat in the Ribble estuary, in north-west England, a site of international importance for wading birds, were bought for reclamation in 1978. The conservation interest would have been largely destroyed and in 1979, after the threat of a compulsory purchase order by the Nature Conservancy Council, the site was sold to the nation for £1.75m, a cost considerably greater than the purchase price the previous year and providing a large profit for one speculator.

On the Wash, a public inquiry was held in 1980 over plans to reclaim 80 ha of salt marsh, part of a much larger proposal. Planning permission was refused because of the strength of the conservation case, which argued that the cost to society of reclaiming 80 ha of salt marsh would be in the region of £300 000, the benefits accruing entirely to the landowner.

Recognition of the importance of salt marshes has led to severe restrictions being imposed on their development in some areas, for instance in the United States (Bradley and Armstrong, 1972) and New Zealand (Chapman, 1974b). Despite some successes for the conservation cause, however, many small reclamations are carried out with little or no control and this steady attrition of saltmarsh habitat may eventually threaten internationally important sites.

7.2 Reclamation for industry

The flat nature of estuarine land, the availability of water for waste disposal and the close proximity to the sea for import and export of materials have long made the intertidal area a prime target for reclamation for urban and industrial development (Fig. 7.2). Cities such as Venice, Amsterdam, Boston, Buenos Aires and much of London have been built on reclaimed marshes (Valiela and Vince, 1976). Many of the important salt marshes which remain, such as those of the east coast of the United States or south-east England, are close to large centres of population, so increasing the threats of industrial development. For example, by 1974, only 6 % remained of the 2400 ha of the intertidal area present in the early

Figure 7.2   Many salt marshes have been reclaimed for industry. This oil refinery complex is at Shellhaven in the Thames estuary. Salt marsh is retained (foreground) and is still of value for wildlife. Some 3.5 % of the world population of Brent geese (*Branta bernicla*) winter in this general area of the Thames estuary.

nineteenth century in the Tees estuary in north-east England (Evans *et al.*, 1979). The extent of this reclamation is illustrated in Fig. 7.3. Where unspoilt marsh abuts industrialized land, the conservation interest may remain high, for instance wading birds may find secure roosting places on industrial tips, as in the Thames estuary (Prater, 1981). The Tees estuary remains an important site for waders, though further planned reclamation makes its future look somewhat bleak (Prater, 1981).

The leisure industry also threatens salt marshes, especially with the development of marinas, which both reclaim salt marsh and cause increased disturbance and damage on the remaining area (Fig. 7.4). Of greater significance, though, are the planned development of estuaries for reservoirs, tidal power production, airports, or flood prevention. Many estuaries, including the larger British ones, and associated salt marshes are threatened by such schemes. A tidal barrage to generate electricity, with associated reclamation, has been proposed for the Severn estuary, while a planned barrage to prevent flooding in the Scheldt estuary of the Nether-

F

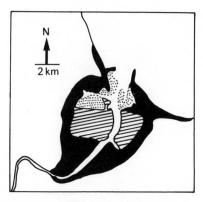

Figure 7.3   Reclamation in the Tees estuary, north-east England. Shaded area, reclaimed before 1960, much after 1930; cross-hatched, reclaimed 1960–1975; stippled, further reclamation planned. Adapted from Evans *et al.*, 1979.

Figure 7.4   A marina development, Canvey Island, Essex. Salt marsh is retained in the foreground, but the disturbance is very high at weekends and during the summer. The reclaimed salt marsh, behind the sea wall, is used as a rubbish tip and provides rich feeding for scavenging gulls and crows.

lands will destroy 60% of the 14.5 km^2 of salt marsh (Smies and Huiskes, 1981). Reservoirs have been planned for the English estuaries of the Dee, Morecambe Bay and Wash, while it has been proposed to develop Maplin Sands at the mouth of the Thames estuary as London's third airport, together with an associated seaport. The John F. Kennedy International Airport of New York stands on reclaimed salt marsh. Prater (1981) details the British schemes and discusses the potential harm they may do to bird populations.

7.3 Pollution

Many estuaries are heavily industrialized, while others are surrounded by intensively farmed land, so that pollution is a particular problem. The intertidal zone is a convenient place to dispose of effluent, frequently with little or no treatment, on the assumption that the sea has an infinite capacity for receiving wastes. Estuaries will also receive wastes from discharges throughout the river catchment and the effluent may be organic, inorganic or directly toxic in nature. Pollution with sewage is a major problem in coastal areas, especially in the United States. Valiela *et al.* (1975) treated plots of *Spartina alterniflora* on the Great Sippewissett Marsh, Massachusetts, with a high-nitrogen fertilizer, made from sewage sludge. Growth of *S. alterniflora* was stimulated to such an extent that other plants were eliminated from the area. Other organisms, though, may benefit from the addition of organic material and nutrients with sewage. Sewage increases the productivity of the intertidal zone, so increasing the potential for wading birds, and it has been suggested that salt marshes could be used for the final "polishing" of effluents, the vegetation removing nitrogen and phosphorus before the waste water enters the sea. The sewage and industrial outfalls in the Forth estuary, particularly waste grain from the discharges of whisky distilleries, attract very large populations of sea duck (Campbell, 1978), though with the improvement in effluent quality, many of the duck have dispersed.

Associated with the effluents are many toxic substances, some of which accumulate in tissues. In the experiment on the Great Sippewissett Marsh, mentioned above, the *Spartina alterniflora* accumulated high levels of cadmium, lead and zinc (Banus *et al.*, 1975). Parslow (1975) has shown how the body load of mercury increases through the winter in waders feeding in the Wash, and is lost while the birds are on their high Arctic breeding grounds. Accumulating toxic chemicals may affect behaviour or reproductive output of those organisms not directly killed by contamination. The effects of pollution on intertidal invertebrates are described by

Hart and Fuller (1979), while a general account of pollution is provided by Mason (1981).

Many salt marshes are at risk from oil pollution and those situated in estuaries with oil refineries are polluted with effluents or spillages quite frequently (Hall *et al.*, 1978, Long and Vandermeulen, 1979, Sanders *et al.*, 1980). The responses of saltmarsh vegetation to oil pollution have been studied by Baker (1971, 1979), Cowell (1969), Cowell and Baker (1969) and Lee *et al.* (1981). Oil becomes very easily trapped within vegetation, where it can be persistent. In a review of some 20 single oil spillages on salt marshes, Baker (1979) concluded that the vegetation recovered well. The most toxic oils were the light crudes and their products, those oils with the smaller molecules. Smothering by heavy oils could cause the death of plants, and mortality was not reduced by methods of cleaning the vegetation, while associated trampling may itself cause damage.

Baker (1979) conducted a valuable series of experiments on simulating the effects of successive spillages of crude oil. Plots within replicated, randomized blocks either received no oil (controls) or were sprayed, to be covered with a light oil film, at 2, 4, 8 or 12 successive monthly intervals. The initial effect was a yellowing of the vegetation, with leaf death, while ensuing growth took place from beneath the soil or from protected growing points. Traces of the oily dead leaves remained for up to five years in a *Juncus maritimus* plot, but had largely disappeared within a year from the *Spartina anglica* plot. Four successive monthly oilings appeared to be critical for the survival of most species, and severe die-back, exposing much mud, occurred with 8–12 sprayings. The upper salt marsh was less affected because the resistant species *Agrostis stolonifera* and *Oenanthe lachenalii* were able to invade. In the *Puccinellia maritima* and *Juncus maritimus* communities, the effects of oiling were still apparent after a decade. Baker (1979) recognized five groups of salt marsh plants in relation to suscepti- bility to oil pollution (Table 7.1).

The effects on a salt marsh of an oil refinery effluent in Southampton Water have also been described by Baker (1979). Large areas of *Spartina anglica* died after two effluent outfalls became operational, mainly due to light oilings from the outfall and from accidental spillages. With an improvement in the effluent quality from 1972, the pioneer species *Salicornia* began quickly to recolonize, with a slower invasion of *Spartina anglica*.

Saltmarsh animals are also affected by oil spills. Lee *et al.* (1981) added heavy fuel oil in autumn to a Georgia salt marsh and recorded three responses in the macro-invertebrates. No population changes occurred in

Table 7.1 The susceptibility of saltmarsh plants to oil pollution.

Group 1 (very susceptible)	Seedlings and annual pioneer species, such as *Salicornia* spp. and *Suaeda maritima*.
Group 2 (susceptible)	Filamentous green algae; *Halimione portulacoides* and *Juncus maritimus*.
Group 3 (intermediate)	Perennials recovering from up to four successive light oilings, but declining on further oiling, e.g. *Spartina anglica*, *Puccinellia maritima*, *Festuca rubra*.
Group 4 (resistant)	Fast growing, mat-forming species such as *Agrostis stolonifera* and *Agropyron pungens* which compete successfully with species damaged by oil. Rosette species with underground storage organs, such as *Armeria maritima* and *Plantago maritima*, are also resistant.
Group 5 (very resistant)	*Oenanthe lachenalii*, an umbellifer, which maintains a small population within the saltmarsh community and invariably responds to heavy oiling by putting out fresh shoots.

fiddler crabs (*Uca pugnax*), oysters (*Crassostrea virginica*) and mussels (*Modiolus demissus*). Periwinkles (*Littorina irrorata*) were killed by the oil, but a larval settlement on the marsh in spring resulted in recolonization. An increase in mud snails (*Nassarius obsoletus*) occurred, as individuals immigrated from adjacent areas to scavenge on dead snails.

7.4 Conservation

The value of salt marshes and the threats to them have been outlined in the preceding pages of this chapter. Being a transitional habitat, salt marsh will always be scarce relative to other habitats. This is so even in an island like Britain, which, with a highly indented coastline, is relatively well endowed with salt marsh. In Britain, tidal flats, salt marsh, sand dunes and vegetated shingle occur in the ratios 5:1:1:0.5 with some 40 500 ha of salt marsh (Ranwell, 1979). The distribution of salt marshes in England and Wales is shown in Fig. 7.5 and it can be seen that over 25% is found in south-east England. We can compare this with the extent of some other British habitats to emphasize the scarceness of the saltmarsh resource:

reservoirs	15 400 ha
salt marsh	40 500 ha
chalk downland	40 500 ha
roadside verges	210 000 ha
ancient woodland	300 000 ha
upland moorland	1 200 000 ha
plantation woodland	1 700 000 ha

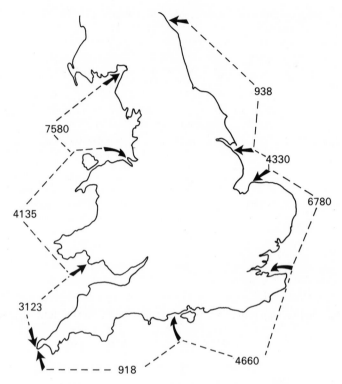

Figure 7.5   Regional distribution of salt marsh (ha) in England and Wales.

Some 70% of this salt marsh is contained within sites listed in the Nature Conservation Review (Ratcliffe, 1977) as of national importance for nature conservation in Britain, but in reality very few of forty or more sites described as containing an area of salt marsh receive protection. The area of salt marsh protected in National and Local Nature Reserves amounts to only 5030 ha. Many of the better salt marshes occur within areas of international importance for waterfowl and should be designated by the U.K. Government as protected areas under the Ramsar Convention on Wetlands of International Importance as Waterfowl Habitat, which Britain signed in 1973. All of the 19 wetland sites designated are, however, already protected by conservation organizations and many key waterfowl sites containing significant salt marsh, such as the Solway Firth, the Wash and Morecambe Bay, remain unprotected, presumably because of their potential for future development. The Netherlands has similarly designated under the Ramsar Convention only those sites which enjoy protection for other reasons (Saeijs and Baptist, 1980).

The management of salt marsh does not require the same involvement as other seral communities such as reedswamps or heathland; new salt marsh often forms along the seaward edge of existing marsh, while coastal defences ensure the maintenance of high marsh, the transition to tidal woodland now being extremely rare. Nevertheless, management of salt marsh may be advisable, particularly in relation to grazing, to improve the sward, and to control the excessive growth of *Spartina*.

Grazing

Many salt marshes are regularly grazed by livestock and, in the past, many more were. Grazing influences the vegetation by trampling, by manuring, which adds nutrients, and by selective feeding. Some species such as *Salicornia europaea*, *Puccinellia maritima* and *Armeria maritima* are favoured by grazing, whereas other species, such as *Aster tripolium*, *Spartina anglica* and *Limonium vulgare*, are harmed (Beeftink, 1977). Sheep grazing can convert a high level *Spartina* marsh to one dominated by *Puccinellia maritima*. In general, prostrate herbs and grasses are favoured at the expense of coarse grasses and upright herbs and, as in the case of meadows and downland, the cessation of grazing will lead to a decrease in floral diversity. *Aster tripolium* is able to survive in a hemicryptophyte state in grazed pastures and can reproduce vegetatively by detachable axillary buds (Ranwell, 1961).

In North American marshes, *Distichlis spicata* is widespread in grazed conditions, but is absent from adjacent ungrazed areas (Shanholtzer, 1974). Reimold *et al.* (1975*b*) showed a 70% reduction in a grazed *S. alterniflora–D. spicata* marsh as compared to an ungrazed one. Production doubled when no grazing took place for a year.

Salt marshes are also grazed by wild animals, such as muskrat (*Ondatra zibethicus*) and snow geese (*Anser caerulescens*) in North America, with wigeon (*Anas penelope*) and brent geese (*Branta bernicla*) important in Western Europe. Snow geese grazing on salt marshes in North Carolina, U.S.A., removed, by consumption or uprooting, 58% of the below-ground biomass of vegetation, and plant cover was reduced in the spring following grazing (Smith and Odum, 1981). On these marshes, *Scirpus robusta* recovered more rapidly than *Distichlis spicata* or *Spartina* spp. Snow geese are also important modifiers of habitat on their Arctic breeding grounds (Chapter 3). The intertidal area of Essex, S.E. England, supports 30% of

Figure 7.6 Brent geese (*Branta bernicla*) feeding on reclaimed saltmarsh pasture, Colne estuary, Essex. Brent geese breed in the high Arctic, where the unpredictable climate often results in poor breeding success, with marked fluctuations in population. Because of this the species has enjoyed protection on its wintering grounds for many years and, for a wild goose, has become relatively confiding, as witnessed in its feeding adjacent to a housing estate in this picture. Protection and a succession of good breeding seasons has boosted the population, while the wholesale ploughing up of saltmarsh pastures is forcing the birds to feed on cereal fields in late winter, when natural foods have been exhausted. This, in turn, is leading to pressure to allow shooting of the geese. A far preferable approach is to provide secure refuges of grazing pasture in the major estuaries. The small loss in agricultural output (of surplus grains) will be far outweighed by the pleasure the refuges will give to a conservation-minded public.

the world population of dark-bellied brent goose (*Branta bernicla bernicla*) (Fig. 7.6). On their arrival in autumn the geese feed on intertidal beds of *Zostera* and when these are depleted they move to *Enteromorpha* salt marsh and in recent years finally to cereal fields (Charman, 1979), where they may significantly reduce yields on a local scale (Deans, 1979). Any loss of the intertidal mudflats and salt marsh in this area, which is threatened with development, could force more of the geese to feed on cereals, thus increasing demands for the control of this important population of a very attractive bird.

Studies in the Bridgwater Bay area of south-west England have shown that wigeon (duck which graze in tightly packed flocks) preferred to feed on swards composed of *Puccinellia maritima* and *Agrostis tenuis*. The sward is, however, being invaded by the rank and tussocky *Festuca rubra*, and sheep, which graze the salt marsh in spring after the ducks have left, could not be stocked at sufficient density to prevent the spread of *F. rubra* (Cadwalladr *et al.*, 1972). Experimental mowing in September prevented the *F. rubra* from developing a tussocky growth, such that the entire area became suitable for grazing (Cadwalladr and Morley, 1974), thus increasing the carrying capacity of the National Nature Reserve for wigeon.

Spartina invasion and die-back

The rapid invasion of intertidal areas by *Spartina anglica* (see Chapter 3) is posing problems in areas where recreational amenities or nature conservation are the prime uses of land. *Spartina* overgrows the mudflats and renders them useless for feeding by waders, who also dislike roosting in the tussocky growth.

Taylor and Burrows (1968) report how 1000 *Spartina* plants were transferred from Dorset to the head of the Dee estuary in 1928 to accelerate land reclamation. A second planting of 3500 cuttings was carried out in the following year. *Spartina* is now the most vigorous primary colonizer in the Dee, producing almost pure swards as it colonizes the foreshore. It has also rapidly invaded the established mixed marsh. Many other estuaries are suffering similar invasion by *Spartina* and herbicides are being extensively used to control the spread on amenity beaches in north-west England.

In some salt marshes, particularly those in southern England where the hybrid *Spartina* was first introduced, extensive die-back is occurring, leaving exposed soils subject to increased erosion (see page 67).

7.5 Conclusion

Salt marshes are a wild and beautiful component of coastal lands and they and their inhabitants make fascinating ecosystems to study. Comparatively little is known as yet about the processes occurring in salt marshes and their importance to adjacent ecosystems. When examined superficially, salt marshes appear rather simple, but closer investigation reveals tremendous diversity of form and process, which makes it unwise, at present, to extrapolate knowledge gained at one site to other marshes. Some facets of study, such as the cycling of nutrients or the export of materials, are in a rapid state of flux, the ideas established during the 1960s being challenged during the 1970s. Clearly, a great deal more research is required.

Yet salt marsh is a scarce resource and a dwindling and threatened one. It is essential for us to conserve what little salt marsh remains to us and to fight vigorously for its protection.

REFERENCES

Abd. Aziz, S. A. (1979) *A study of nitrogen cycling in a coastal salt marsh ecosystem.* Ph.D. thesis, University of Essex, Colchester.

Abd. Aziz, S. A. and Nedwell, D. B. (1979) Microbial nitrogen transformations in the salt marsh environment. In: *Ecological Processes in Coastal Environments* (eds. R. L. Jefferies and A. J. Davy), Blackwell, Oxford, pp. 385–398.

Abram, J. W. and Nedwell, D. B. (1978a) Inhibition of methanogenesis by sulphate reducing bacteria competing for transferred hydrogen. *Arch. Microbiol.* **117**, 89–92.

Abram, J. W. and Nedwell, D. B. (1978b) Hydrogen as a substrate for methanogenesis and sulphate reduction in anaerobic salt marsh sediment. *Arch. Microbiol.* **117**, 93–97.

Adam, P. (1976) The occurrence of bryophytes on British salt marshes. *J. Bryol.* **9**, 265–274.

Adam, P. (1978) Geographical variation in British salt marsh vegetation. *J. Ecol.* **66**, 339–366.

Adam, P. (1981) The vegetation of British (UK) saltmarshes. *New Phytol.* **88**, 143–196.

Adams, S. M. and Angelovic, J. W. (1970) Assimilation of detritus and its associated bacteria by three species of estuarine animals. *Chesapeake Sci.* **11**, 249–254.

Admiralty (1980) *Tide Tables I. European Waters.* Hydrographer to the Navy, Taunton.

Ahmad, I., Wainwright, S. J. and Stewart, G. R. (1981) The solute and water relations of *Agrostis stolonifera* ecotypes differing in their salt tolerance. *New Phytol.* **87**, 615–629.

Albert, R. (1975) Salt regulation in halophytes. *Oecologia* **21**, 57–71.

Anderson, C. E. (1974) A review of structure in several North Carolina salt marsh plants. In: *Ecology of Halophytes* (eds. R. J. Reimold and W. H. Queen), Academic Press, New York, pp. 307–344.

Anderson, C. M. and Treshow, M. (1980) A review of environmental and genetic factors that affect height in *Spartina alterniflora* (salt marsh cord grass). *Estuaries* **3**, 168–176.

Armstrong, W. (1967). The oxidizing activity of roots in waterlogged soils. *Physiol. Pl.* **20**, 920–926.

Armstrong, W. (1976) Waterlogged soils. In: *Environment and Plant Ecology* (ed. J. R. Etherington), Wiley, London, pp. 181–218.

Atkinson, L. P. and Hall, J. R. (1976) Methane distribution and production in the Georgia salt marsh. *Est. Coast. Mar. Sci.* **4**, 677–686.

Baker, J. M. (1971) Studies on salt marsh communities. In: *The Ecological Effects of Oil Pollution on Littoral Communities* (ed. E. B. Cowell), Applied Science Publishers, Barking, pp. 16–101.

Baker, J. M. (1979) Responses of salt marsh vegetation to oil spills and refinery effluents. In: *Ecological Processes in Coastal Environments* (eds. R. L. Jefferies and A. J. Davy), Blackwell, Oxford, pp. 529–542.

Balba, M. T. and Nedwell, D. B. (1982) Microbial metabolism of acetate, propionate and butyrate in anoxic sediment from Colne Point salt marsh, Essex, U.K. *J. Gen. Microbiol.* **128**, 1415–1422.

Banat, I. M., Lindstrom, E. B., Nedwell, D. B. and Balba, M. T. (1981) Evidence of co-existence of two distinct functional groups of sulphate-reducing bacteria in salt marsh sediment. *Appl. Environ. Microbiol.* **42**, 985–992.

139

Banus, M. D., Valiela, I. and Teal, J. M. (1975) Lead, zinc and cadmium budgets in experimentally enriched salt marsh ecosystems. *Est. Coast. Mar. Sci.* **3**, 421–430.

Bartholomew, G. A. and Cade, T. J. (1963) The water economy of land birds. *Auk* **80**, 504–539.

Beeftink, W. G. (1966) Vegetation and habitat of the salt marshes and beach plains in the south-western part of the Netherlands. *Wentia* **15**, 83–108.

Beeftink, W. G. (1977) The coastal salt marshes of western and northern Europe: an ecological and phytosociological approach. In: *Wet coastal ecosystems* (ed. V. J. Chapman), Elsevier, Amsterdam, pp. 109–155.

Beeftink, W. G., Daane, M. C., van Liere, J. M. and Nieuwenhuize, J. (1977) Analysis of estuarine soil gradients in salt marshes of the south-western Netherlands with special reference to the Scheldt estuary. *Hydrobiologia* **52**, 93–106.

Beeftink, W. G. (1979) The structure of salt marsh communities in relation to environmental disturbances. In: *Ecological Processes in Coastal Environments* (eds. R. L. Jefferies and A. J. Davy), Blackwell, Oxford, pp. 77–94.

Bell, S. S. (1979) Short- and long-term variation in a high marsh meiofauna community. *Est. Coast. Mar. Sci.* **9**, 331–350.

Bell, S. S. (1980). Meiofauna-macrofauna interactions in a high salt marsh habitat. *Ecol. monogr.* **50**, 487–505.

Berner, R. A. (1980) *Early Diagenesis; A Theoretical Approach.* Princeton Univ. Press, Princeton.

Bernstein, L. (1964) Effects of salinity on mineral composition and growth of plants. In: *Plant Analysis and Fertilizer Problems* IV (ed. C. Bould), W. R. Humphrey Press, New York, pp. 25–45.

Bidwell, R. G. S. (1979) *Plant Physiology.* 2nd edn., Collier Macmillan, New York.

Biscoe, P. V., Clark, J. A., Gregson, K., McGowan, M., Monteith, J. L. and Scott, R. K. (1975a) Barley and its environment. I. Theory and practice. *J. appl. Ecol.* **12**, 227–247.

Biscoe, P. V., Scott, R. K. and Monteith, J. L. (1975b) Barley and its environment. III. Carbon budget of the stand. *J. appl. Ecol.* **12**, 269–293.

Bloom, A. L. (1967) Pleistocene shorelines: a new test of isostasy. *Geol. Soc. Amer. Bull.* **78**, 1477–1494.

Boorman, L. A. (1971) Studies in salt marsh ecology with special reference to the genus *Limonium. J. Ecol.* **59**, 103–120.

Boorman, L. A. and Ranwell, D. S. (1977) *Ecology of Maplin Sands and the Coastal Zones of Suffolk, Essex and North Kent.* Institute of Terrestrial Ecology, Cambridge.

Bowen, G. D. (1980) Misconceptions, concepts and approaches to rhizosphere biology. In: *Contemporary Microbial Ecology* (eds. D. C. Ellwood, J. H. Hedger, M. J. Latham, J. M. Lynch and J. H. Slater), Academic Press, London, pp. 283–304.

Boyle, C. D. and Patriquin, D. G. (1981) Carbon metabolism of *Spartina alterniflora* in relation to that of associated nitrogen fixing bacteria. *New Phytol.* **89**, 275–288.

Bradley, E. H. and Armstrong, J. M. (1972) A description and analysis of coastal zone and shoreland management programs in the United States. *Univ. Mich. Sea Grant Tech. Rep.* **20**, 1–426.

Bradshaw, J. S. (1968) Environmental parameters and marsh foraminifera. *Limnol. Oceanogr.* **13**, 26–38.

Brafield, A. E. and Newell, G. E. (1961) The behaviour of *Macoma balthica* (L.). *J. Mar. Biol. Ass. U.K.* **41**, 81–87.

Brereton, A. J. (1971) The structure of the species populations in the initial stages of salt marsh succession. *J. Ecol.* **59**, 321–338.

Breteler, R. J., Teal, J. M., Giblin, A. E. and Valiela, I. (1981) Trace element enrichments in decomposing litter of *Spartina alterniflora. Aquat. Bot.* **11**, 111–120.

Brinkhuis, B. H. and Jones, R. F. (1976) The ecology of temperate salt marsh fucoids. II. In situ growth of transplanted *Ascophyllum nodosum* ecads. *Mar. Biol.* **34**, 339–348.

Broome, S. W., Woodhouse, W. W. and Seneca, E. D. (1975a) The relationship of mineral nutrients to growth of *Spartina alterniflora* in North Carolina. I. Nutrient status of plants and soils in natural stands. *Soil Sci. Soc. Amer. Proc.* **39**, 295–301.

Broome, S. W., Woodhouse, W. W. and Seneca, E. D. (1975b)The relationship of mineral nutrients to growth of *Spartina alterniflora* in North Carolina. II. The effects of N, P and Fe fertilizers. *Soil Sci. Soc. Amer. Proc.* **39**, 301–307.

Brownell, P. F. (1979) Sodium as an essential micronutrient element for plants and its possible role in metabolism. *Adv. Bot. Res.* **7**, 118–219.

Burg, M. E., Tripp, D. R. and Rosenberg, E. S. (1980) Plant associations and primary productivity of Nisqually salt marsh on southern Puget Sound, Washington, U.S.A. *Northwest Sci.* **54**, 222–236.

Burke, M. V. and Mann, K. H. (1974) Productivity and production: biomass ratios of bivalve and gastropod populations in an eastern Canadian estuary. *J. Fish. Res. Bd. Canada* **31**, 167–177.

Burkholder, P. R. and Bornside, G. H. (1957) Decomposition of marsh grass by aerobic marine bacteria. *Bull. Torrey bot. Club* **84**, 366–383.

Butler, R. J. (1978) *Salt marsh morphology and the evolution of Colne Point in Essex, England.* Ph.D. thesis, Queen Mary College, University of London.

Butler, R. J., Greensmith, J. T. and Wright, L. W. (1981) Shingle spits and salt marshes in the Colne Point area of Essex: a geomorphological study. *Occasional Papers in Geography* (ed. P. E. Ogden), Queen Mary College, University of London, London, No. 18.

Cadbury, C. J. (1973) Bird populations of the Wash. *Cambridge Bird Club Rep. for 1972* **46**, 33–39.

Cadwalladr, D. A. and Morley, J. V. (1974) Further experiments on the management of saltings pasture for wigeon (*Anas penelope* L.) conservation at Bridgwater Bay National Nature Reserve, Somerset. *J. appl. Ecol.* **11**, 461–466.

Cadwalladr, D. A., Owen, M., Morley, J. V. and Cook, R. S. (1972) Wigeon (*Anas penelope* L.) conservation and salting pasture management in Bridgwater Bay National Nature Reserve, Somerset. *J. appl. Ecol.* **9**, 417–425.

Calow, P. (1981) *Invertebrate Biology. A Functional Approach.* Croom Helm, London.

Campbell, L. H. (1978) Patterns of distribution and behaviour of flocks of seaducks wintering at Leith and Musselburgh, Scotland. *Biol. Conserv.* **14**, 111–124.

Cammen, L. M. (1976) Accumulation rate and turnover time of organic carbon in salt marsh sediment. *Limnol. Oceanogr.* **20**, 1012–1015.

Cammen, L. M., Seneca, E. D. and Copeland, B. J. (1974) Animal colonization of salt marshes artificially established on dredge spoil. *Univ. N. Carolina Sea Grant Publ. UNC-SG-74-15.*

Cammen, L. M., Seneca, E. D. and Stroud, L. M. (1980) Energy flow through the fiddler crabs *Uca pugnax* and *U. minax* and the marsh periwinkle *Littorina irrorata* in a North Carolina salt marsh. *Am. Midl. Nat.* **103**, 238–250.

Champeau, A. (1979) Les responses des copepodes (Crustaces) aux changements des conditions physico-chimiques dans les eaux temporaires Camarguaises Provencales et Corses. In: *Ecological Processes in Coastal Environments* (eds. R. L. Jefferies and A. J. Davy), Blackwell Scientific Publications, Oxford, pp. 285–293.

Chapman, V. J. (1959) Studies in salt marsh ecology. IX. Changes in salt marsh vegetation at Scolt Head Island. *J. Ecol.* **47**, 619–639.

Chapman, V. J. (1974a) *Salt Marshes and Salt Deserts of the World.* 2nd edn, J. Cramer Verlag, Bremerhaven.

Chapman, V. J. (1974b). Coastal zone management in New Zealand. *Coastal Zone Manage. J.* **1**, 333–345.

Chapman, V. J. (1976) *Coastal vegetation.* 2nd edn. Pergamon Press, Oxford.

Chapman, V. J. (1977) Introduction. In: *Wet Coastal Ecosystems* (ed. V. J. Chapman), Elsevier, Amsterdam, pp. 1–39.

Charman, K. (1979) Feeding ecology and energetics of the dark-bellied brent goose (*Branta bernicla bernicla*) in Essex and Kent. In: *Ecological Processes in Coastal Environments* (eds. R. L. Jefferies and A. J. Davy), Blackwell, Oxford, pp. 451–465.

Christian, R. R. and Wetzel, R. L. (1981) Interaction between substrate, microbes, and consumers of *Spartina* detritus in estuaries. In: *Estuarine Interactions* (ed. M. L. Wiley), Academic Press, New York, pp. 93–113.

Clapham, A. R., Tutin, T. G. and Warburg, E. F. (1962) *Flora of the British Isles*. 2nd edn., Cambridge University Press, Cambridge.

Coles, S. M. (1979) Benthic microalgal populations on intertidal sediments and their role as precursors to salt marsh development. In: *Ecological Processes in Coastal Environments* (eds. R. L. Jefferies and A. J. Davy), Blackwell, Oxford, pp. 25–42.

Colinvaux, P. A. (1973) *Introduction to Ecology*. Wiley International, New York.

Cooper, A. W. (1974) Salt marshes. In: *Coastal Ecological Systems of the U.S*. Vol. 2. (eds. H. T. Odum, B. J. Copeland and E. A. McMahon), The Conservation Foundation, Washington D.C., pp. 55–98.

Coull, B. C., Bell, S. S., Savory, A. M. and Dudley, B. W. (1979) Zonation of meiobenthic copepods in a south-eastern United States salt marsh. *Est. Coast. Mar. Sci*. **9**, 181–188.

Cowell, E. B. (1969) The effects of oil pollution on salt marsh communities in Pembrokeshire and Cornwall. *J. appl. Ecol*. **6**, 133–142.

Cowell, E. B. and Baker, J. M. (1969) Recovery of a salt marsh in Pembrokeshire, S. Wales, from pollution by crude oil. *Biol. Conserv*. **1**, 291–295.

Critchley, C. (1982) Stimulation of photosynthetic electron transport in a salt-tolerant plant by high chloride concentrations. *Nature* **298**, 483–485.

Croghan, P. C. (1958) The mechanism of osmotic regulation in *Artemia salina* (L.). *J. Exp. Biol*. **35**, 243–249.

Cruz, A. A. de la (1973) The role of tidal marshes in the productivity of coastal waters. *Assoc. S.E. Biol. Bull*. **20**, 147–156.

Cruz, A. A. de la and Gabriel, R. C. (1974) Caloric, elemental, and nutritive changes in decomposing *Juncus roemerianus* leaves. *Ecology* **55**, 882–886.

Daiber, F. C. (1982) *Animals of the Tidal Marsh*. Van Nostrand Reinhold Co., New York.

Dainty, J. (1979) The ionic and water relations of plants which adjust to a fluctuating saline environment. In: *Ecological Processes in Coastal Environments* (eds. R. L. Jefferies and A. J. Davy), Blackwell, Oxford, pp. 201–210.

Dalby, D. H. (1970) The salt marshes of Milford Haven, Pembrokeshire. *Fld. Std*. **3**, 297–330.

Daly, M. A. and Mathieson, A. C. (1981) Nutrient fluxes within a small north temperate salt marsh. *Mar. Biol*. **61**, 337–344.

Day, J. W., Smith, W. G., Wagner, P. R. and Stowe, W. C. (1973) Community structure and carbon budget of a salt marsh and shallow bay estuarine system in Louisiana. Louisiana State University Center for Wetland Resources Publ. LSU-SG-72-04, Baton Rouge, 79 pp.

Deans, I. R. (1979) Feeding of brent geese on cereal fields in Essex and observations on the subsequent loss of yield. *Agro-Ecosystems* **5**, 283–288.

DeLaune, R. D. and Patrick, W. H. Jr. (1980) Rate of sedimentation and its role in nutrient cycling in a Louisiana salt marsh. In: *Estuarine and Wetland Processes with Emphasis on Modelling* (eds. P. Hamilton and K. B. Macdonald), Plenum Press, New York, pp. 401–412.

De Niro, M. and Epstein, S. (1978) Influences of diet on the distribution of carbon isotopes in animals. *Geochim. Cosmochim. Acta* **42**, 495–506.

De Oliveira, F. E. C. and Fletcher, A. (1980) Taxonomic and ecological relationships between rocky-shore and salt marsh populations of *Pelvetia canaliculata* (Phaeophyta) at Four Mile Bridge, Anglesey (Wales) U.K. *Bot. Mar*. **23**, 409–418.

Downes, R. W. (1969) Differences in transpiration rates between tropical and temperate grasses under controlled conditions. *Planta* **88**, 261–273.

Dozier, H. L., Markley, M. H. and Llewellyn, L. M. (1948) Muskrat investigations on the Blackwater National Wildlife Refuge, Maryland, 1941–45. *J. Wildl. Mgmt*. **12**, 177–190.

Drake, B. G. and Read, M. (1981) Carbon dioxide assimilation, photosynthetic efficiency, and respiration of a Chesapeake Bay salt marsh. *J. Ecol.* **69**, 405–423.

Dunn, R. (1981) *The effects of temperature on the photosynthesis, growth and productivity of Spartina townsendii (sensu lato) in controlled and natural environments.* Ph.D. thesis, University of Essex, Colchester.

Dury, G. (1972) *The Face of the Earth.* Pelican, Harmondsworth.

Elderfield, H. and Hepworth, A. (1975) Diagenesis, metals and pollution in estuaries. *Mar. Pollut. Bull.* **5**, 85–87.

Evans, P. R., Herdson, D. M., Knights, P. J. and Pienkowski, M. W. (1979) Short-term effects of reclamation of part of Seal Sands, Teesmouth, on wintering waders and shelduck. I. Shorebird diets, invertebrate densities, and impact of predation on the invertebrates. *Oecologia* **41**, 183–206.

Fenchel, T. (1970) Studies on the decomposition of organic detritus derived from the turtle grass *Thalassia testudinum. Limnol. Oceanogr.* **15**, 14–20.

Fenchel, T. and Blackburn, T. H. (1979) *Bacteria and Mineral Cycling.* Academic Press, London.

Fenchel, T. and Harrison, P. (1976) The significance of bacterial grazing and mineral cycling for the decomposition of particulate detritus. In: *The Role of Terrestrial and Aquatic Organisms in Decomposition Processes* (eds. J. M. Anderson and A. Macfadyen), Blackwell, Oxford, pp. 285–299.

Flowers, T. J., Troke, P. F. and Yeo, A. R. (1977) The mechanism of salt tolerance in halophytes. *Ann. Rev. Pl. Physiol.* **28**, 89–121.

Foster, W. A. and Moreton, R. B. (1981) Synchronization of activity rhythms with the tide in a salt marsh collembolan *Anurida maritima. Oecologia* **50**, 265–270.

Foster, W. A. and Treherne, J. E. (1975) The distribution of an intertidal aphid, *Pemphigus trehernei* Foster, on marine salt marshes. *Oecologia* **21**, 141–155.

Foster, W. A. and Treherne, J. E. (1976a) The effects of tidal submergence on an intertidal aphid, *Pemphigus trehernei* Foster. *J. anim. Ecol.* **45**, 291–301.

Foster, W. A. and Treherne, J. E. (1976b) Insects of marine salt marshes: problems and adaptations. In: *Marine Insects* (ed. L. Cheng), Elsevier, Amsterdam, pp. 5–42.

Frey, R. W. and Basan, P. B. (1978) North American coastal salt marshes. In: *Coastal Sedimentary Environments* (ed. R. A. Davis), Springer-Verlag, Berlin, pp. 109–169.

Fuller, R. J. (1982) *Bird Habitats in Britain.* T. & A. D. Poyser, Calton.

Gallagher, J. L. and Daiber, F. C. (1974) Primary production of edaphic algal communities in a Delaware salt marsh. *Limnol. Oceanogr.* **19**, 390–395.

Gallagher, J. L., Pfeiffer, W. J. and Pomeroy, L. R. (1976) Leaching and microbial utilization of dissolved organic carbon from leaves of *Spartina alterniflora. Est. Coast. Mar. Sci.* **4**, 467–471.

Gallagher, J. L., Reimold, R. J., Linthurst, R. A. and Pfeiffer, W. J. (1980) Aerial production, mortality, and mineral accumulation-export dynamics in *Spartina alterniflora* and *Juncus roemerianus* plant stands in a Georgia salt marsh. *Ecology* **61**, 303–312.

Giurgevich, J. R. and Dunn, E. L. (1978) Seasonal patterns of CO_2 and water vapour exchange of *Juncus roemerianus* Scheele in a Georgia salt marsh. *Amer. J. Bot.* **65**, 502–510.

Glooschenko, W. A. (1978) Above-ground biomass and vascular plants in a subarctic James Bay salt marsh. *Can. Field Nat.* **92**, 30–37.

Godshalk, G. L. and Wetzel, R. G. (1978) Decomposition of aquatic angiosperms. III. *Zostera marina* L. and a conceptual model of decomposition. *Aquat. Bot.* **5**, 329–354.

Goldberg, E. D. (1963) The oceans as a chemical system. In: *The Sea* (ed. M. N. Hill) **2**, 3–25. Interscience, London.

Goodman, P. J., Braybrooks, E. M. and Lambert, J. M. (1959). Investigations into "die-back" in *Spartina townsendii.* I. The present status of *S. townsendii* in Britain. *J. Ecol.* **47**, 651–677.

Goodman, P. J. and Williams, W. T. (1961) Investigations into "die-back" in *Spartina townsendii* agg. III. Physiological correlates of "die-back". *J. Ecol.* **49**, 391–398.

Gosselink, J. G. and Kirby, C. J. (1974) Decomposition of salt marsh grass *Spartina alterniflora* Loisel. *Limnol. Oceanogr.* **19**, 825–832.

Gosselink, J. G., Odum, E. P. and Pope, R. M. (1974) *The value of the tidal marsh*. Louisiana State University Center for Wetland Resources, Publ. LSU-SG-74-03, Baton Rouge.

Gray, A. J. (1972) The ecology of Morecambe Bay. V. The salt marshes of Morecambe Bay. *J. appl. Ecol.* **9**, 207–220.

Gray, A. J. and Bunce, R. G. H. (1972) The ecology of Morecambe Bay. VI. Soils and vegetation of the salt marshes: a multivariate approach. *J. appl. Ecol.* **9**, 221–234.

Gray, A. J., Parsell, R. J. and Scott, R. (1979) The genetic structure of plant populations in relation to the development of salt marshes. In: *Ecological Processes in Coastal Environments* (eds. R. L. Jefferies and A. J. Davy), Blackwell, Oxford, pp. 43–64.

Gray, A. J. and Scott, R. (1977a) Biological flora of the British Isles. *Puccinellia maritima* (Huds.) Parl. *J. Ecol.* **65**, 699–716.

Gray, A. J. and Scott, R. (1977b) The ecology of Morecambe Bay. VII. The distribution of *Puccinellia maritima*, *Festuca rubra* and *Agrostis stolonifera* in the salt marshes. *J. appl. Ecol.* **14**, 229–241.

Green, J. (1968) *The Biology of Estuarine Animals*. Sidgwick and Jackson, London.

Greenhalgh, M. E. (1971) The breeding bird communities of Lancashire salt marshes. *Bird Study* **18**, 199–212.

Greensmith, J. T. and Tucker, E. V. (1966) Morphology and evolution of inshore shell ridges and mud-mounds on modern intertidal flats at Bradwell, Essex. *Proc. Geol. Assoc.* **77**, 329–346.

Greenway, H. and Munns, R. (1980) Mechanisms of salt tolerance in nonhalophytes. *Ann. Rev. Pl. Physiol.* **31**, 149–190.

Greenway, H. and Osmond, C. B. (1972) Salt responses of enzymes from species differing in salt tolerance. *Pl. Physiol.* **49**, 256–259.

Gregor, J. W. (1946) Ecotypic differentiation. *New Phytol.* **45**, 254–270.

Gribble, F. C. (1976) Census of black-headed gull colonies in England and Wales in 1973. *Bird Study* **23**, 139–149.

Haines, E. B. (1976a) Stable carbon isotope ratios in the biota, soils and tidal water of a Georgia salt marsh. *Est. Coast. Mar. Sci.* **4**, 609–616.

Haines, E. B. (1976b) Relation between the stable carbon isotope composition of fiddler crabs, plants and soils in a salt marsh. *Limnol. Oceanogr.* **21**, 833–880.

Haines, E. B. (1977) The origins of detritus in Georgia salt marsh estuaries. *Oikos* **29**, 254–260.

Haines, E. B. (1979) Interactions between Georgia salt marshes and coastal waters: a changing paradigm. In: *Ecological Processes in Coastal and Marine Systems* (ed. R. J. Livingston), Plenum, New York, pp. 35–46.

Hall, C. A. S., Howarth, R. W., Moore, B. and Vorosmarty, C. J. (1978) Environmental impacts of industrial energy systems in the coastal zone. *A. Rev. Energy* **3**, 395–475.

Hargrave, B. T. (1976) The central role of invertebrate faeces in sediment decomposition. In: *The Role of Terrestrial and Aquatic Organisms in Decomposition Processes* (eds. J. M. Anderson and A. Macfadyen), Blackwell, Oxford, pp. 301–321.

Harris, C. B. (1977) Sedimentology and geomorphology. In: *North Bull Island, Dublin Bay—A Modern Coastal Natural History*. (ed. D. W. Jeffrey), Royal Dublin Society, Dublin, pp. 13–25.

Harrison, P. G. (1977) Decomposition of macrophyte detritus in seawater: effects of grazing by amphipods. *Oikos* **28**, 165–169.

Harrison, P. G. and Mann, K. H. (1975) Detritus formation from eelgrass (*Zostera marina* L.): the relative effects of fragmentation, leaching and decay. *Limnol. Oceanogr.* **20**, 924–934.

Hart, C. J. and Fuller, S. L. H. (1979) *Pollution Ecology of Estuarine Invertebrates*. Academic Press, New York.

Heath, D. J. (1974) Seasonal changes in frequency of the "yellow" morph of the isopod,

Sphaeroma rugicauda. Heredity **32**, 299–307.

Heath, D. J. (1975) Geographical variation in populations of the polymorphic isopod, *Sphaeroma rugicauda. Heredity* **35**, 99–107.

Heinle, D. R. and Flemer, D. A. (1976) Flows of materials between poorly flooded tidal marshes and an estuary. *Mar. Biol.* **35**, 359–373.

Henriksen, K. and Jensen, A. (1979) Nitrogen mineralization in a salt marsh ecosystem dominated by *Halimione portulacoides.* In: *Ecological Processes in Coastal Environments* (eds. R. L. Jefferies and A. J. Davy), Blackwell, Oxford, pp. 373–384.

Heydemann, B. (1979) Responses of animals to spatial and temporal environmental heterogeneity within salt marshes. In: *Ecological Processes in Coastal Environments* (eds. R. L. Jefferies and A. J. Davy), Blackwell Scientific Publications, Oxford, pp. 145–163.

Hill, A. E. (1967*a*) Ion and water transport in *Limonium.* I. Active transport by leaf gland cells. *Biochim. Biophys. Acta* **135**, 454–460.

Hill, A. E. (1967*b*) Ion and water transport in *Limonium.* II. Short-circuit analysis. *Biochim. Biophys. Acta* **135**, 461–465.

H.M.S.O. (1975) *Food From Our Own Resources.* H.M.S.O., London.

H.M.S.O. (1979) *Farming and the Nation.* H.M.S.O., London.

Hoffnagle, J. R. (1980) Estimates of vascular plant primary production in a West Coast, U.S.A., salt marsh–estuary ecosystem. *Northwest Sci.* **54**, 68–79.

Holland, A. F., Zingmark, R. G. and Dean, J. M. (1974) Quantitative evidence concerning the stabilization of sediments by marine benthic diatoms. *Mar. Biol.* **27**, 191–196.

Houghton, R. A. and Woodwell, G. M. (1980) The Flax Pond ecosystem study: exchanges of carbon dioxide between a salt marsh and the atmosphere. *Ecology* **61**, 1434–1445.

Howarth, R. W. and Teal, J. M. (1980) Energy flow in a salt marsh ecosystem: the role of reduced inorganic sulphur compounds. *Amer. Nat.* **116**, 862–872.

Howes, B. L., Howarth, R. W., Teal, J. M. and Valiela, I. (1981) Oxidation-reduction potentials in a salt marsh: spatial patterns and interactions with primary production. *Limnol. Oceanogr.* **26**, 350–360.

Hsaio, T. C. (1973) Plant responses to water stress. *Ann. Rev. Pl. Physiol.* **24**, 519–570.

Hubbard, J. C. E. (1965) *Spartina* marshes in southern England. VI. Pattern of invasion in Poole Harbour. *J. Ecol.* **53**, 799–813.

Hubbard, J. C. E. (1969) Light in relation to tidal immersion and the growth of *Spartina townsendii* (*s.l.*). *J. Ecol.* **57**, 795–804.

Hunt, H. W., Cole, C. V., Klein, D. A. and Coleman, D. C. (1977) A simulation model for the effect of predation on bacteria in continuous culture. *Microb. Ecol.* **3**, 259–278.

Hussey, A. (1980) *The net primary production of an Essex salt marsh, with particular reference to Puccinellia maritima.* Ph.D. thesis, University of Essex, Colchester.

Hussey, A. and Long, S. P. (1982) Seasonal changes in weight of above- and below-ground vegetation and dead plant material in a salt marsh at Colne Point, Essex. *J. Ecol.* **70**, 757–772.

Jefferies, R. L. (1977) The vegetation of salt marshes at some coastal sites in Arctic North America. *J. Ecol.* **65**, 661–672.

Jefferies, R. L., Davy, A. J. and Rudmik, T. (1979*a*) The growth strategies of coastal halophytes. In: *Ecological Processes in Coastal Environments* (eds. R. L. Jefferies and A. J. Davy), Blackwell, Oxford, pp. 243–268.

Jefferies, R. L., Davy, A. J. and Rudmik, T. (1981) Population biology of the salt marsh annual *Salicornia europaea. J. Ecol.* **69**, 17–32.

Jefferies, R. L., Jensen, A. and Abraham, K. F. (1979*b*) Vegetational development and the effect of geese on vegetation at La Pérouse Bay, Manitoba. *Can. J. Bot.* **57**, 1439–1450.

Jefferies, R. L. and Perkins, N. (1977) The effects on the vegetation of the additions of inorganic nutrients to salt marsh soils at Stiffkey, Norfolk. *J. Ecol.* **65**, 867–882.

Jennings, D. H. (1968) Halophytes, succulence and sodium in plants—a unified theory. *New Phytol.* **67**, 899–911.

Jensen, A. (1980) Seasonal changes in near IR reflectance ratio and standing crop biomass in a salt marsh community dominated by *Halimione portulacoides*. *New Phytol.* **86**, 57–68.

Johannes, R. E. and Satomi, M. (1967) Measuring organic matter retained by aquatic invertebrates. *J. Fish. Res. Bd. Canada* **24**, 2467–2471.

Johnen, B. G. and Sauerbeck, D. R. (1977) A tracer technique for measuring growth, mass and microbial breakdown of plant roots. *Ecol. Bull.* **25**, 366–373.

Jones, J. D. (1972) *Comparative Physiology of Respiration*. Edward Arnold, London.

Joosse, E. N. G. (1976) Littoral apterygotes (Collembola and Thysanura). In: *Marine Insects* (ed. L. Cheng), North-Holland Publishing Company, Amsterdam, pp. 151–186.

Kaplan, W. A., Teal, J. M. and Valiela, I. (1977) Denitrification in salt marsh sediments: evidence for seasonal temperature selection among populations of denitrifiers. *Microb. Ecol.* **3**, 193–204.

Kay, Q. O. N. and Rajanvipart, P. (1977) Salt marsh ecology and trace-metal studies. In: *Problems of a Small Estuary* (eds. A. Nelson-Smith and E. M. Bridges), Institute of Marine Studies, Swansea, pp. 2/1–2/15.

Kershaw, K. A. (1976) The vegetational zonation of the East Pen Island salt marshes, Hudson Bay. *Can. J. Bot.* **54**, 5–13.

Kestner, F. J. T. and Inglis, C. C. (1956) A study of erosion and accretion during cyclic changes in an estuary and their effect on reclamation of marginal land. *J. Agric. Eng. Res.* **1**, 63–67.

Kinne, O. (1964) The effects of temperature and salinity on marine and brackish water animals. II. Salinity and temperature–salinity combinations. *Oceanogr. Mar. Biol. Ann. Rev.* **2**, 281–339.

Kirby, C. J. and Gosselink, J. G. (1976) Primary production in a Louisiana Gulf Coast *Spartina alterniflora* marsh. *Ecology* **57**, 1052–1059.

Kofoed, L. H. (1975) The feeding biology of *Hydrobia ventrosa* (Montague). I. The assimilation of different components of food. *J. exp. mar. Biol. Ecol.* **19**, 1–9.

Kruczynski, W. L., Subrahmanyam, C. B. and Drake, S. H. (1979) Studies on the plant community of a north Florida salt marsh. II. Nutritive value and decomposition. *Bull. mar. Sci.* **28**, 707–715.

Kuenzler, E. J. (1961a) Phosphorus budget of a mussel population. *Limnol. Oceanogr.* **6**, 400–415.

Kuenzler, E. J. (1961b) Structure and energy flow of a mussel population in a Georgia salt marsh. *Limnol. Oceanogr.* **6**, 191–204.

Larcher, W. (1975) *Physiological Plant Ecology*. Springer-Verlag, Berlin.

Lee, J. J. (1980) A conceptual model of marine detrital decomposition and the organisms associated with the process. In: *Advances in Aquatic Microbiology, Vol. 2* (eds. M. R. Droop and H. W. Jannasch), Academic Press, London, pp. 257–291.

Lee, R. F., Dornseif, B., Gonsoulin, F., Tenore, K. and Hanson, R. (1981) Fate and effects of a heavy fuel oil spill on a Georgia salt marsh. *Marine Environ. Res.* **5**, 125–143.

Leeks, G. (1979) Mudlarks in the Essex marshes. *Geogr. Mag.* **51**, 665–669.

Letzsch, W. S. and Frey, R. W. (1980) Erosion of salt marsh tidal creek banks, Sapelo Island, Georgia, U.S.A. *Senckenb. Marit.* **12**, 201–212.

Levinton, J. S. and Lopez, G. R. (1977) A model of renewable resources and limitation of deposit-feeding benthic populations. *Oecologia* **31**, 177–190.

Lieth, H. and Whittaker, R. H. (eds.) (1975) *The Primary Production of the Biosphere*. Springer-Verlag, New York.

Linthurst, R. A. (1980) A growth comparison of *Spartina alterniflora* ecophenes under aerobic and anaerobic conditions. *Amer. J. Bot.* **67**, 883–887.

Linthurst, R. A. and Reimold, R. J. (1978a) An evaluation of methods for estimating the net aerial primary production of estuarine angiosperms. *J. appl. Ecol.* **15**, 919–931.

Linthurst, R. A. and Reimold, R. J. (1978b) Estimated net aerial primary productivity for selected estuarine angiosperms in Maine, Delaware and Georgia. *Ecology* **59**, 945–955.

Livingstone, D. A. (1963). Chemical composition of rivers and lakes. U.S. Geological Survey Professional Paper 440-G.

Lockwood, A. P. M. (1963) *Animal Body Fluids and their Regulation*. Heinemann, London.

Lockwood, A. P. M. and Inman, C. B. E. (1979) Ecophysiological responses of *Gammarus duebeni* to salinity fluctuations. In: *Ecological Processes in Coastal Environments* (eds. R. L. Jefferies and A. J. Davy), Blackwell Scientific Publications, Oxford, pp. 269–284.

Long, B. F. N. and Vandermeulen, J. H. (1979) Impact of clean-up efforts on an oiled salt marsh (Ile Grande) in North Brittany, France. *Spill Technol. Newsletter* **4**, 218–229.

Long, S. P. (1976) C_4 photosynthesis in cool temperate climates, with reference to Spartina townsendii (s.l.) in Britain. Ph.D. thesis, University of Leeds, Leeds.

Long, S. P. (1981) Measurement of photosynthetic gas exchange. In: *Techniques in Bioproductivity and Photosynthesis* (eds. J. Coombs and D. O. Hall), Pergamon, Oxford, pp. 25–36.

Long, S. P. and Incoll, L. D. (1979) The prediction and measurement of photosynthetic rate of *Spartina townsendii (sensu lato)* in the field. *J. appl. Ecol.* **16**, 879–891.

Long, S. P., Incoll, L. D. and Woolhouse, H. W. (1975) C_4 photosynthesis in plants from cool temperate regions, with particular reference to *Spartina townsendii*. *Nature* **257**, 622–624.

Long, S. P. and Woolhouse, H. W. (1979) Primary production in *Spartina* marshes. In: *Ecological Processes in Coastal Environments* (eds. R. L. Jefferies and A. J. Davy), Blackwell, Oxford, pp. 333–352.

Longbottom, M. R. (1970) The distribution of *Arenicola marina* (L.) with particular reference to the effect of particle size and organic matter of the sediments. *J. exp. mar. Biol. Ecol.* **5**, 138–157.

Lopez, G. R. and Levinton, J. S. (1978) The availability of microorganisms attached to sediment particles as food for *Hydrobia ventrosa* Montagu (Gastropoda:Prosobranchia). *Oecologia* **32**, 236–275.

Lopez, G. R., Levinton, J. S. and Slobodkin, L. B. (1977) The effect of grazing by the detritivore *Orchestia grillus* on *Spartina* litter and its associated microbial community. *Oecologia* **30**, 111–127.

Lüttge, E. (1975) Salt glands. In: *Ion Transport in Plant Cells and Tissues* (eds. D. A. Baker and J. L. Hall), North-Holland, Amsterdam, pp. 335–376.

Luxton, M. (1967a) The ecology of salt marsh Acarina. *J. anim. Ecol.* **36**, 257–277.

Luxton, M. (1967b) The zonation of salt marsh Acarina. *Pedobiologia* **7**, 55–66.

Lynch, J. J., O'Neil, T. and Lay, D. W. (1947) Management significance of damage by geese and muskrats to Gulf Coast marshes. *J. Wildl. Mgmt.* **11**, 50–76.

Maccubbin, A. E. and Hodson, R. E. (1980) Mineralization of detrital lignocelluloses by salt marsh sediment microflora. *Appl. Environ. Microbiol.* **40**, 735–740.

Macdonald, K. B. (1977) Plant and animal communities of Pacific North American salt marshes. In: *Wet Coastal Ecosystems* (ed. V. J. Chapman), Elsevier, Amsterdam, pp. 167–191.

Mann, K. H. (1979) Nitrogen limitations on the productivity of *Spartina* marshes, *Laminaria* kelp beds and higher trophic levels. In: *Ecological Processes in Coastal Environments* (eds. R. L. Jefferies and A. J. Davy), Blackwell, Oxford, pp. 363–370.

Marinucci, A. C. (1982) Trophic importance of *Spartina alterniflora* production and decomposition to the marsh-estuarine ecosystem. *Biol. Conserv.* **22**, 35–58.

Marsden, I. D. (1973) The influence of salinity and temperature on the survival and behaviour of the isopod *Sphaeroma rugicauda* from a salt marsh habitat. *Mar. Biol.* **21**, 75–85.

Mason, C. F. (1974) Mollusca. In: *Biology of Plant Litter Decomposition* (eds. C. H. Dickinson and G. J. F. Pugh), Academic Press, London, pp. 555–591.

Mason, C. F. (1977) *Decomposition*. Edward Arnold, London.

Mason, C. F. (1981) *Biology of Freshwater Pollution*. Longman, London.

McCaffrey, R. J. (1977) *A record of the accumulation of sediment and trace metals in a*

Connecticut, USA, salt marsh. Ph.D. Dissertation, Yale University, New Haven.

McClung, C. R. and Patriquin, D. G. (1980) Isolation of a nitrogen-fixing *Campylobacter* sp. from the roots of *Spartina alterniflora. Can. J. Microbiol.* **26**, 881–886.

McGovern, T. A., Laber, L. J. and Gram, B. C. (1979) Characteristics of the salts secreted by *Spartina alterniflora* Loisel and their relation to estuarine production. *Est. Coast. Mar. Sci.* **9**, 351–356.

Meadows, P. S. and Campbell, J. I. (1978) *An Introduction to Marine Science.* Blackie, Glasgow.

Meadows, P. S. and Reid, A. (1966) The behaviour of *Corophium volutator* (Crustacea, Amphipoda). *J. Zool., Lond.* **150**, 387–399.

Mechalas, B. J. (1974) Pathways and environmental requirements for biogenic gas production in the oceans. In: *Natural Gases in Marine Sediments* (ed. I. R. Kaplan), Plenum Press, New York, pp. 12–25.

Meesenburg, H. (1971) Spartinas kolonisation og udbredelse langs Ho Bugt. *Geografisk Tidskrift* **71**, 37–45.

Mendelssohn, I. A. and Seneca, E. D. (1980) The influence of soil drainage on the growth of salt marsh cordgrass *Spartina alterniflora* in North Carolina. *Est. Coast. Mar. Sci.* **11**, 27–40.

Meyers, P. A. and Dolphin, D. R. (1977) A system for determining economic loss associated with estuary degradation. *Coastal Zone Manage. J.* **3**, 385–404.

Milner, C. and Hughes, R. E. (1968) *Methods for the Measurement of the Primary Production of Grassland.* IBP Handbook No. 6, Blackwell, Oxford.

Moll, R. A. (1977) Phytoplankton in a temperate-zone salt marsh: Net production and exchanges with coastal waters. *Mar. Biol.* **42**, 109–118.

Montague, C. L., Bunker, S. M., Haines, E. B., Pace, M. L. and Wetzel, R. L. (1981) Aquatic macroconsumers. In: *The Ecology of a Salt Marsh* (eds. L. R. Pomeroy and R. G. Wiegert), Springer-Verlag, New York, pp. 69–85.

Mooring, M. T., Cooper, A. W. and Seneca, E. D. (1971) Seed germination response and evidence for height ecophenes in *Spartina alterniflora* from North Carolina. *Amer. J. Bot.* **58**, 48–55.

Morris, J. T. (1982) A model of growth responses by *Spartina alterniflora* to nitrogen limitation. *J. Ecol.* **70**, 25–42.

Morrison, S. J. and White, D. C. (1980) Effects of grazing by estuarine gammaridean amphipods on the microbiota of allochthonous detritus. *Appl. environ. Microbiol.* **40**, 659–671.

Natural Environment Research Council (1976) *The Wash water storage scheme feasibility study; a report on the ecological studies.* N.E.R.C., London.

Nedwell, D. B. and Abram, J. W. (1978) Bacterial sulphate reduction in relation to sulphur geochemistry in two contrasting areas of salt marsh sediment. *Est. Coast. Mar. Sci.* **6**, 341–351.

Newell, R. C. (1965) The role of detritus in the nutrition of two marine deposit-feeders, the prosobranch *Hydrobia ulvae* and the bivalve *Macoma balthica. Proc. zool. Soc. Lond.* **144**, 25–45.

Newell, R. C. (1970) *Biology of Intertidal Animals.* Elek, London.

Nixon, S. W. (1980) Between coastal marshes and coastal waters—a review of twenty years of speculation and research on the role of salt marshes in estuarine productivity and water chemistry. In: *Estuarine and Wetland Processes with Emphasis on Modelling* (eds. P. Hamilton and K. B. Macdonald), Plenum Press, New York, pp. 437–525.

Nixon, S. W. and Oviatt, C. A. (1973) Ecology of a New England salt marsh. *Ecol. Monogr.* **43**, 463–498.

Odum, E. P. and de la Cruz, A. A. (1967) Particulate organic detritus in a Georgia salt marsh-estuarine ecosystem. In: *Estuaries* (ed. G. H. Lauff). AAAS, Washington.

Odum, W. E. and Fanning, M. E. (1973) Comparisons of the productivity of *Spartina alterniflora* and *Spartina cynosuroides* in Georgia coastal marshes. *Bull. Ga. Acad. Sci.* **31**, 1–12.

Odum, W. E., Fisher, J. S. and Pickral, J. C. (1979) Factors controlling the flux of particulate organic carbon from estuarine wetlands. In: *Ecological Processes in Coastal and Marine Systems* (ed. D. J. Livingston), Plenum, New York, pp. 69–80.

Odum, W. E. and Heald, E. J. (1975) The detritus based food web of an estuarine mangrove community. In: *Estuarine Research, Vol. 1* (ed. L. E. Cronin), Academic Press, New York, pp. 265–286.

Odum, E. P. and Smalley, A. E. (1959) Comparison of population energy flow of a herbivorous and a deposit-feeding invertebrate in a salt marsh ecosystem. *Proc. Nat. Acad. Sci., Washington* **45**, 617–622.

O'Keefe, C. W. (1972) Marsh production: a summary of the literature. *Contrib. Mar. Sci.* **16**, 163–181.

Olney, P. J. S. (1963) The food and feeding habits of the teal *Anas crecca* L. *Proc. Zool. Soc. Lond.* **140**, 169–210.

Osmond, C. B. and Greenway, H. (1972) Salt responses of carboxylation enzymes from species differing in salt tolerance. *Pl. Physiol.* **49**, 260–263.

Othman, S. B. (1980) *The distribution of salt marsh plants and its relation to edaphic factors with particular reference to Puccinellia maritima and Spartina townsendii.* Ph.D. thesis, University of Essex, Colchester.

Pace, M. L., Shimmel, S. and Darley, W. M. (1979) The effect of grazing by a gastropod, *Nassarius obsoletus*, on the benthic microbial community of a salt marsh mudflat. *Est. Coast. Mar. Sci.* **9**, 121–134.

Packham, J. R. and Liddle, M. J. (1970) The Cefni salt marsh, Anglesey, and its recent development. *Fld. Std.* **3**, 331–356.

Parslow, J. L. F. (1975) Mercury in waders from the Wash. *Environ. Pollut.* **5**, 295–304.

Patrick, W. H. Jr. and DeLaune, R. D. (1976) Nitrogen and phosphorus utilization by *Spartina alterniflora* in a salt marsh in Barataria Bay, Louisiana. *Est. Coast. Mar. Sci.* **4**, 59–64.

Patriquin, D. G. (1978) Factors affecting nitrogenase activity (acetylene-reducing activity) associated with excised roots of the emergent halophyte *Spartina alterniflora* Loisel. *Aquat. Bot.* **4**, 193–210.

Pellenbarg, R. E. (1978) *Spartina alterniflora* litter and the aqueous surface microlayer in the salt marsh. *Est. Coast. Mar. Sci.* **6**, 187–195.

Perkins, E. J. (1974) The marine environment. In: *Biology of Plant Litter Decomposition* (eds. C. H. Dickinson and G. J. F. Pugh), Academic Press, London, pp. 683–721.

Perkins, E. J. (1974a) *The Biology of Estuaries and Coastal Waters.* Academic Press, New York.

Pestrong, J. S. (1965) The development of drainage patterns on tidal marshes. *University of Stanford Studies in Geological Science* **10**, 1–87.

Pethick, J. S. (1974) The distribution of salt pans on tidal marshes. *J. Biogeogr.* **1**, 57–62.

Pfeiffer, W. J. and Wiegert, R. G. (1981) Grazers on *Spartina* and their predators. In: *The Ecology of a Salt Marsh* (eds. L. R. Pomeroy and R. G. Wiegert), Springer-Verlag, New York, pp. 87–112.

Polderman, P. J. G. and Polderman-Hall, R. A. (1980) Algal communities in Scottish salt marshes, U.K. *Phycol. J.* **15**, 59–72.

Prater, A. J. (1981) *Estuary Birds of Britain and Ireland.* T. and A. D. Poyser, Calton.

Price, C. H. and Russell-Hunter, W. D. (1975) Behavioural and physiological aspects of water relations in the high littoral snail *Melampus bidentatus* Say. *Biol. Bull.* **149**, 442–443.

Queen, W. H. (1977) Human uses of salt marshes. In: *Wet Coastal Ecosystems* (ed. V. J. Chapman), Elsevier, Amsterdam, pp. 363–368.

Ranwell, D. S. (1961) *Spartina* salt marshes in southern England. I. The effects of sheep grazing at the upper limits of *Spartina* marsh in Bridgwater Bay. *J. Ecol.* **49**, 325–340.

Ranwell, D. S. (1964) *Spartina* salt marshes in southern England. III. Rates of establishment, succession and nutrient supply at Bridgwater Bay, Somerset. *J. Ecol.* **52**, 95–105.

Ranwell, D. S. (1972) *Ecology of Salt Marshes and Sand Dunes.* Chapman and Hall, London.

Ranwell, D. S. (1979) Strategies for the management of coastal systems. In: *Ecological Processes in Coastal Environments* (eds. R. L. Jefferies and A. J. Davy), Blackwell, Oxford, pp. 515–527.

Ranwell, D. S. and Downing, B. M. (1959) Brent goose winter feeding pattern and *Zostera* resources at Scolt Head Island, Norfolk. *Anim. Behav.* **7**, 42–56.

Ratcliffe, D. A. (ed.) (1977) *A Nature Conservation Review*. Cambridge University Press, Cambridge.

Reidenbaugh, T. G. and Banta, W. C. (1980) Origin and effects of *Spartina alterniflora* wrack in a Virginia (U.S.A.) salt marsh. *Gulf Res. Rep.* **6**, 393–402.

Reimold, R. J. (1972) The movement of phosphorus through the salt marsh cord grass, *Spartina alterniflora* Loisel. *Limnol. Oceanogr.* **17**, 606–611.

Reimold, R. J. (1977) Mangals and salt marshes of eastern United States. In: *Wet Coastal Ecosystems* (ed. V. J. Chapman), Elsevier, Amsterdam, pp. 157–166.

Reimold, R. J., Gallagher, J. L., Linthurst, R. A. and Pfeiffer, W. J. (1975a) Detritus production in coastal salt marshes. In: *Estuarine Research 1* (ed. L. E. Cronin), Academic Press, New York, pp. 217–228.

Reimold, R. J., Linthurst, R. A. and Wolf, P. L. (1975b) Effects of grazing on a salt marsh. *Biol. Conserv.* **8**, 105–125.

Richards, F. J. (1934) The salt marshes of the Dovey estuary. IV. The rates of accretion, horizontal extension and scarp erosion. *Ann. Bot.* **48**, 225–259.

Rozema, J. and Blom, B. (1977) Effects of salinity and inundation on the growth of *Agrostis stolonifera* and *Juncus gerardii*. *J. Ecol.* **65**, 213–222.

Rozema, J., Gude, H. and Pollak, G. (1981) An ecophysiological study of the salt secretion of four halophytes. *New Phytol.* **89**, 201–217.

Ruber, E., Gillis, G. and Montagna, P. A. (1981) Production of dominant emergent vegetation and of pool algae on a northern Massachusetts, U.S.A., salt marsh. *Bull. Torrey Bot. Club* **108**, 180–188.

Russell, E. W. (1961) *Soil Conditions and Plant Growth*. 9th edn., Longman, London.

Saeijs, H. L. F. and Baptist, H. J. M. (1980) Coastal engineering and European wintering wetland birds. *Biol. Conserv.* **17**, 63–83.

St. Omer, L. and Schlesinger, W. H. (1980) Regulation of sodium chloride in *Jaumea carnosa* (Asteraceae), a salt marsh species, and its effect on leaf succulence. *Amer. J. Bot.* **67**, 1448–1454.

Sanders, H. L., Grassle, J. F., Hampson, G. R., Morse, L. S., Garner-Price, S. and Jones, C. C. (1980) Anatomy of an oil spill: long-term effects from the grounding of the barge *Florida* off West Falmouth, Massachusetts. *J. Mar. Res.* **38**, 265–280.

Sauerbeck, D. R. and Johnen, B. G. (1977) Root formation and decomposition during plant growth. *Soil Organic Matter Studies* **1**, 141–148.

Schelski, C. L. and Odum, E. P. (1961) Mechanisms maintaining high productivity in Georgia estuaries. *Proc. Gulf. Carib. Fish. Inst.* **14**, 75–80.

Scoffin, T. P. (1970) The trapping and binding of subtidal carbonate sediments by marine vegetation in Bimini Lagoon, Bahamas. *J. sedim. Petrol.* **40**, 249–273.

Seneca, E. D. (1974) Stabilization of coastal dredge spoil with *Spartina alterniflora*. In: *Ecology of Halophytes* (eds. R. J. Reimold and W. H. Queen), Academic Press, New York, pp. 463–474.

Senior, E., Lindstrom, E. B., Banat, I. M. and Nedwell, D. B. (1982) Sulphate reduction and methanogenesis in the sediment of a salt marsh on the east coast of the United Kingdom. *Appl. Environ. Microbiol.* **43**, 987–996.

Settlemyre, J. L. and Gardner, L. R. (1977) Suspended sediment flux through a salt marsh drainage basin. *Est. Coast. Mar. Sci.* **5**, 653–663.

Shanholtzer, G. G. (1974) Relationship of vertebrates to salt marsh plants. In: *Ecology of Halophytes* (eds. R. J. Reimold and W. H. Queen), Academic Press, New York, pp. 463–474.

Shea, M. L., Warren, R. S. and Niering, W. A. (1975) Biochemical and transplantation studies of the growth form of *Spartina alterniflora* on Connecticut salt marshes. *Ecology* **56**, 461–466.

Sherr, B. F. and Payne, W. J. (1978) Effect of the *Spartina alterniflora* root-rhizome system on salt marsh soil denitrifying bacteria. *Appl. Environ. Microbiol.* **35**, 724–729.

Smalley, A. E. (1960) Energy flow of a salt marsh grasshopper population. *Ecology* **41**, 672–677.

Smies, M. and Huiskes, A. H. I. (1981) Holland's Eastern Scheldt estuary barrier scheme: some ecological considerations. *Ambio* **10**, 158–165.

Smith, D. L., Bird, C. J., Lynch, K. D. and McLachlan, J. (1980) Angiosperm productivity in two salt marshes of Minas Basin, Nova Scotia, Canada. *Proc. N.S. Inst. Sci.* **30**, 109–118.

Smith, T. J. and Odum, W. E. (1981) The effects of grazing by snow geese on coastal salt marshes. *Ecology* **62**, 98–106.

Solav'ev, V. A. (1969) Distribution of cations in plants depending on the degree of salinization of the substrate. *Fiziol. Rast.* **16**, 498–504.

Steers, J. A. (1964) *The Coastline of England and Wales.* 2nd edn., Cambridge University Press, Cambridge.

Steers, J. A. (1977) Physiography. In: *Wet Coastal Ecosystems* (ed. V. J. Chapman), Elsevier, Amsterdam, pp. 31–60.

Stewart, G. R., Larher, F., Ahmad, I. and Lee, J. A. (1979) Nitrogen metabolism and salt-tolerance in higher plant halophytes. In: *Ecological Processes in Coastal Environments* (eds. R. L. Jefferies and A. J. Davy), Blackwell, Oxford, pp. 211–228.

Storey, R., Ahmad, N. and Wyn Jones, R. G. (1979) Taxonomic and ecological aspects of the distribution of glycinebetaine and related compounds in plants. *Oecologica* **27**, 319–332.

Storey, R. and Wyn Jones, W. G. (1978) Salt stress and comparative physiology in the Gramineae. I. Ion relations of two salt- and water-stressed barley cultivars, California Mariout and Arimar. *Aust. J. Pl. Physiol.* **5**, 801–816.

Tanner, W. F. (1960) Florida coastal classification. *Trans. Gulf Coast Assoc. Geol. Soc.* **10**, 259–266.

Tansley, A. G. (1949) *The British Islands and their Vegetation.* Cambridge University Press, Cambridge.

Taylor, M. C. and Burrows, E. M. (1968) Studies on the biology of *Spartina* in the Dee estuary, Cheshire. *J. Ecol.* **56**, 795–809.

Teal, J. M. (1959) Respiration of crabs in Georgia salt marshes and its relation to their ecology. *Physiol. Zool.* **32**, 1–14.

Teal, J. M. (1962) Energy flow in the salt marsh ecosystem of Georgia. *Ecology* **43**, 614–624.

Teal, J. M. and Teal, M. (1969) *The Life and Death of a Salt Marsh.* Little, Brown and Co., Boston.

Tenore, K. R. (1981) Organic nitrogen and caloric content of detritus. I. Utilization by the deposit-feeding polychaete, *Capitella capitata. Est. Coast. Shelf Sci.* **12**, 39–47.

Thayer, G. W., Parker, P. L., Lacroix, M. W. and Fry, B. (1978) The stable isotope ratio of some components of an eelgrass, *Zostera marina* bed. *Oecologia* **35**, 1–12.

The Times (1980) *World Atlas.* Times Newspapers, London.

Tooley, H. (1975) Sea-level changes during the last 9,000 years in north-west England. *Geogr. J.* **141**, 18–42.

Trattner, R. B. and Mattson, C. P. (1976) Nitrogen budget determination in the Hackensack Meadowlands estuary. *J. environ. Sci. Health* **8**, 549–565.

Treherne, J. E. and Foster, W. A. (1977) Diel activity of an intertidal beetle, *Dicheirotrichus gustavi* Crotch. *J. anim. Ecol.* **46**, 127–138.

Treherne, J. E. and Foster, W. A. (1979) Adaptive strategies of air-breathing arthropods from marine salt marshes. In: *Ecological Processes in Coastal Environments* (eds. R. L. Jefferies and A. J. Davy), Blackwell Scientific Publications, Oxford, pp. 165–175.

Turitzin, S. N. and Drake, B. G. (1981) The effect of a seasonal change in canopy structure on the photosynthetic efficiency of a salt marsh. *Oecologia* **48**, 79–84.

Turner, R. E. (1976) Geographic variations in salt marsh macrophyte production: a review *Contrib. Mar. Sci.* **20**, 47–68.

Tutin, T. G., Heywood, V. H., Burges, N. A., Valentine, D. H., Walters, S. M. and Webb, D. A. (1964–1980) *Flora Europaea* Vols. 1–5. Cambridge University Press, Cambridge.

Valiela, I. and Teal, J. M. (1974) Nutrient limitation in salt marsh vegetation. In: *Ecology of Halophytes* (eds. R. J. Reimold and W. H. Queen), Academic Press, New York, pp. 547–563.

Valiela, I. and Teal, J. M. (1979) Inputs, outputs and interconversions of nitrogen in a salt marsh ecosystem. In: *Ecological Processes in Coastal Environments* (eds. R. L. Jefferies and A. J. Davy), Blackwell, Oxford, pp. 399–414.

Valiela, I., Teal, J. M. and Deuser, W. G. (1978) The nature of growth forms in the salt marsh grass *Spartina alterniflora. Amer. Nat.* **112**, 461–470.

Valiela, I., Teal, J. M., Volkmann, S., Shafer, D. and Carpenter, E. J. (1978) Nutrient and particulate fluxes in a salt marsh ecosystem: tidal exchanges and inputs by precipitation and ground water. *Limnol. Oceanogr.* **23**, 798–812.

Valiela, I., Teal, J. M. and Sass, W. J. (1975) Production and dynamics of salt marsh vegetation and the effects of experimental treatment with sewage sludge. *J. appl. Ecol.* **12**, 973–982.

Valiela, I. and Vince, S. (1976) Green borders of the sea. *Oceanus* **19**, 10–17.

Van Raalte, C. D., Valiela, I. and Teal, J. M. (1976) Production of epibenthic salt marsh algae: light and nutrient limitations. *Limnol. Oceanogr.* **21**, 862–872.

Vince, S. W., Valiela, I. and Teal, J. M. (1981) An experimental study of the structure of herbivorous insect communities in a salt marsh. *Ecology* **62**, 1662–1678.

Vlasblom, A. G. and Elgershuizen, J. H. B. W. (1977) Survival and oxygen consumption of *Praunus flexuosus* and *Neomysis integer*, and embryonic development of the latter species, in different temperature and chlorinity combinations. *Neth. J. Sea Res.* **11**, 305–315.

Weir, V. and Bannister, K. E. (1973) The food of the otter in the Blakeney area. *Trans. Norfolk Norwich Nat. Soc.* **22**, 377–382.

Welsh, B. L. (1975) The role of grass shrimp, *Palaemonetes pugio*, in a tidal marsh ecosystem. *Ecology* **56**, 513–530.

Westhoff, V. and Schouten, M. G. C. (1979) The diversity of European coastal ecosystems. In: *Ecological Processes in Coastal Environments* (eds. R. L. Jefferies and A. J. Davy), Blackwell, Oxford, pp. 3–21.

White, D. A., Weis, T. E., Trapani, J. M. and Thien, L. B. (1978) Productivity and decomposition of the dominant salt marsh plants in Louisiana. *Ecology* **59**, 751–759.

Whittaker, R. H. (1975) *Communities and Ecosystems*. 2nd edn. Macmillan, New York.

Widdel, F. and Pfennig, N. (1977) A new anaerobic sporing, acetate oxidizing, sulphate-reducing bacterium, *Desulfotomaculum* (emend.) *acetooxidans. Arch. Microbiol.* **112**, 119–122.

Wiegert, R. G. (1979) Ecological processes characteristic of coastal *Spartina* marshes of the south-eastern U.S.A. In: *Ecological Processes in Coastal Environments* (eds. R. L. Jefferies and A. J. Davy), Blackwell, Oxford, pp. 467–490.

Williams, R. B. (1972) *Plant Productivity in Coastal Waters*, Delaware Academy of Sciences Symposium.

Williams, R. B. and Murdoch, M. B. (1967) The potential importance of *Spartina alterniflora* in conveying zinc, manganese, and iron into estuarine food chains. *Proc. 2nd Natl. Symp. Radioecol.*, U.S.A.E.C., pp. 431–439.

Williams, W. T. and Lambert, J. M. (1959) Multivariate methods in plant ecology. I. Association—analysis in plant communities. *J. Ecol.* **47**, 83–101.

Winter, K. (1979) Photosynthetic and water relationships of higher plants in a saline environment. In: *Ecological Processes in Coastal Environments* (eds. R. L. Jefferies and A. J. Davy), Blackwell, Oxford, pp. 297–331.

Wolff, W. J., van Eeden, M. N. and Lammens, E. (1979) Primary production and import of particulate organic matter on a salt marsh in the Netherlands. *Neth. J. Sea Res.* **13**, 242–255.

Woodwell, G. M., Hall, C. A. and Houghton, R. A. (1977) The Flax Pond ecosystem study: exchanges of carbon in water between a salt marsh and Long Island Sound. *Limnol. Oceanogr.* **22**, 833–838.

Woodwell, G. M., Houghton, R. A., Hall, C. A. S., Whitney, D. E., Moll, R. A. and Juers, D. W. (1979) The Flax Pond ecosystem study: the annual metabolism and nutrient budgets of a salt marsh. In: *Ecological Processes in Coastal Environments* (eds. R. L. Jefferies and A. J. Davy), Blackwell, Oxford, pp. 491–511.

Woodwell, G. M. and Whitney, D. E. (1977) The Flax Pond ecosystem study: exchanges of phosphorus between a salt marsh and the coastal waters of Long Island Sound. *Marine Biology* **41**, 1–6.

Wootton, R. J. (1976) *The Biology of Sticklebacks*. Academic Press, London.

Yaakub, M. H. (1980) *Growth, photosynthesis and mineral nutrition of the halophytes Aster tripolium L. (var. discoideus Reichb.) and Spartina townsendii in response to salinity*. Ph.D. thesis, University of Essex, Colchester.

Yapp, R. H., Johns, D. and Jones, O. T. (1917) The saltmarshes of the Dovey Estuary. II. The saltmarshes. *J. Ecol.* **5**, 65–103.

Index

154

 MAY 1 6 1994

 1987

DISCHARGED
APR 0 3 1994

APR 2 5 1994
DISCHARGED

FEB 1 6 1998 DISCHARGED

DISCHARGED
APR 2 8 2000